CAUSES AND CONSEQUENCES
OF THE
FIRST
WORLD WAR

CAUSES AND CONSEQUENCES

OF THE

FIRST WORLD WAR

STEWART ROSS

CAUSES AND CONSEQUENCES
The First World War
The Second World War
The Arab-Israeli Conflict

Published by Evans Brothers Limited
2A Portman Mansions,
Chiltern Street,
London W1U 6NR
England

First published in paperback in 2003

ISBN 0 237 52568 2

Planning and production by Discovery Books Ltd
Edited by Helena Ramsay
Designed by Ian Winton

CONTENTS

ASSASSINATION AT SARAJEVO

The events that triggered the First World War began with an unlucky mistake. Archduke Franz Ferdinand was heir to the throne of the mighty Austro-Hungarian Empire. In the summer of 1914 he and his wife Sophie made a brave but provocative state visit to the troubled province of Bosnia. On the morning of 28 June terrorists attacked the royal couple in Sarajevo, the Bosnian capital. A bomb blast took the rear wheel off the visitors' car, but left them unharmed.

Later in the day, however, their chauffeur took a wrong turning into a narrow alley and had to stop the car to back out. Scarcely able to believe his luck, teenage assassin Gavrilo Princip stepped forward and shot Franz Ferdinand and Sophie dead.

ASSASSINATION LEADS TO EUROPEAN WAR

Bosnia had once been part of the Turkish Ottoman Empire. As this empire gradually fell apart, new, independent nations such as Greece (1833) and Serbia (1878) came into being. Bosnia, too, broke free of Turkish rule. But instead of getting full independence, she was taken over by Austria-Hungary. This infuriated Bosnian nationalists like Gavrilo Princip. The assassination of Archduke Franz Ferdinand was Princip's dramatic way of telling the government of Austria-Hungary that the Bosnians wanted independence.

Unfortunately, back in Vienna the Austro-Hungarian government saw the assassination as more than just a Bosnian matter. They believed, with some justification, that Princip's terrorist gang had been aided by neighbouring Serbia. The rulers of Austria-Hungary loathed Serbia. When Serbia annexed land during the Balkan wars of 1912-1913, Austria-Hungary felt threatened by its increasing size. It was

The murder that rocked the world: a somewhat fanciful artist's impression of the assassination of Archduke Franz Ferdinand and his wife Sophie in Sarajevo, Bosnia, in the summer of 1914.

also antagonized by Serbia's support for Bosnian nationalists and its close political and ethnic links with Russia. As Austria-Hungary and Russia were rival powers, any ally of Russia's automatically found itself under suspicion from Austria-Hungary.

Vienna decided to use the assassination as an excuse for a showdown with Serbia. Germany, Austria-Hungary's powerful ally, gave the project her full support. On 23 July, 1914 Vienna sent Serbia an ultimatum that, if accepted, would have made Serbia virtually an Austro-Hungarian province. The Serbs had 48 hours to accept it — or face the consequences.

Unwilling to stand by and watch her friends in the Balkans crushed, Russia began mobilizing her armed forces. When Serbia refused to accept all the clauses of the ultimatum, Austria-Hungary declared war at 11 a.m. on 28 July. A chain reaction began two

I foresee that very soon I shall be over-whelmed by the pressure brought upon me and be forced to take extreme measures which will lead to war.

Tsar Nicholas II of Russia in a telegram to his cousin, Kaiser Wilhelm II of Germany, 29 July 1914.

days later when the Tsar of Russia stepped up his preparations. The Germans insisted that he should stop. When he refused, Germany declared war on Russia. France, Russia's ally, mobilized her forces in response. Keen to strike first, Germany declared war on France on 3 August and advanced through neutral Belgium. Britain entered the war the following day to help France and Belgium.

Thus, five short weeks after the Sarajevo assassination, the European powers were at war.

EUROPEAN WAR BECOMES WORLD WAR

Relief at last — the Illustrated London News *welcomes US entry into the First World War on the Allied side in April 1917.*

In Europe, the war was greeted with wild patriotism and an optimistic belief that it would be short-lived and successful. Britain and France declared that within a few weeks the massive Russian forces would crush their enemies into the ground. Even if things did not go well on land, the British argued, their mighty fleet would soon throttle Germany into submission.

For their part, the Germans had been planning a major European war for years. They were sure their well-drilled armies would sweep all before them and end the war in months. Austria-Hungary, confident of crushing Serbia, knew she could rely on German help against Russia.

All forecasts of swift victory proved tragically wrong. By Christmas the forces of both sides were bogged down in murderous trench warfare, dominated by artillery, machine guns and barbed wire. The terrible slaughter dragged on for four and a half years. Shortages, conscription, air raids and a massive increase in government power affected every household in the warring nations. Soldiers from Europe's widespread overseas empires came to fight for their mother countries. Naval warfare took the

The United States: Her Armed Strength

"We are now about to accept gage of battle with this natural foe to liberty, and shall, if necessary, spend the whole force of the nation to check and nullify its pretensions and its power."

—PRESIDENT WILSON ON GERMANY.

fighting over the oceans; colonial campaigns brought it to Africa and the Far East.

Each year fresh countries were sucked into the war. Japan joined the Allies (Britain, France and Russia) in 1914, while the Turks sided with the Central Powers (Germany and Austria-Hungary). This took the fighting into the Middle East, where the Arabs sought freedom from their Turkish overlords. Italy, after nine months of neutrality, became one of the Allies, as did Romania and Greece. Bulgaria teamed up with the Central Powers.

Most Americans regarded what was going on in Europe with a mixture of horror, fascination and relief. Their most powerful feeling was a determination, whatever happened, not to get involved. Before long, however, they realised this was far easier said than done.

During the first two-and-a-half years of war, US economic links with the Allies grew steadily. Over the same period, Germany's naval tactics and ill-judged diplomacy upset American opinion. Finally, in the spring of 1917 the US entered the war on the Allied side.

> The Great European War had become a world war. The general view was that it would be over by Christmas. Our major anxiety was by hook or by crook not to miss it.
>
> Harold Macmillan, the future British Prime Minister, remembering the mood in the country in the late summer of 1914.

WHY DID IT HAPPEN?

As soon as war broke out in 1914, historians and politicians began to ask why it had happened. What had gone wrong? As the fighting spread and casualties mounted, the question became more urgent. To this day no one has come up with a definitive explanation.

During the war and immediately afterwards, three views prevailed. The Allies claimed the war had been 'imposed upon them' by German aggression. For their part, the Germans said that before 1914 they had been gradually encircled by hostile powers and they declared war to avoid being crushed.

Led by Vladimir Lenin, the Russian Communists put forward a third explanation. They called the First World War an 'imperialist struggle'. It was, they believed, the inevitable result of competition between the capitalist nations to dominate the world's markets.

By the 1930s the view of historians in the US and Europe had changed. They said it was unfair and too simple to blame Germany for starting the war.

'A spectre is haunting Europe, the spectre of Communism'. A sentence from the Communist Manifesto *which serves to caption this propaganda poster of 1919. Vladimir Lenin (1870-1924) the leader of Russia's Communist Revolution, labelled the First World War as an 'imperialist struggle'.*

It was more realistic to say that the world had, in the words of British wartime prime minister Lloyd George, 'slithered' into war. The fault lay not with a single country but with the system. Secret diplomacy, alliances, an arms race and a fatal miscalculation brought about a war that no one really wanted.

By the 1980s, with most government documents from the early years of the century available, opinion had changed again. It seemed as if the Allies' post-war view — that Germany had deliberately provoked the war — was quite accurate after all. Believing war inevitable, the leaders of Germany had planned for it — even sought it — sooner rather than later. The longer war was delayed, they calculated, the less chance they had of winning.

CAUSES AND TRIGGERS

Although Germany may have forced the hand of the European powers in the summer of 1914, she did not 'cause' the war. She was not responsible for creating the atmosphere in which war was a probability. The three chapters that follow will examine the different sources of tension in Europe immediately before the First World War.

ALLIANCES AND ENTENTES

The First World War broke out against a background of rivalry between the world's great powers. These powers were, in the first rank, Britain, Germany, France and Russia and the USA. Austria-Hungary, Italy, the Ottoman Empire and Japan were in the second rank. No single power was dominant. The US, for example, had the most dynamic economy, Britain the most powerful navy and Germany the most effective army.

From the 1870s onwards, the powers formed alliances for greater security. The system began in central Europe and gradually spread further afield. By 1914 the US was the only power not connected to the international web of military agreements. The importance of this web was that it made limited war very unlikely. When two great powers went to war, the alliances had a 'domino' effect, bringing others into the conflict. As we saw in the first chapter, this was precisely what happened after Austria-Hungary declared war on Serbia in 1914.

Our policy in regard to Europe ... remains the same, which is, not to interfere in the internal concerns of any of its powers; to consider the government de facto as the legitimate government for us; to cultivate friendly relations with it, and to preserve those relations by a frank, firm and manly policy ....

Part of the 'Monroe Doctrine' as set out by President James Monroe in his Message to Congress, 2 December 1823. The Doctrine guided US foreign policy until the close of the century.

THE UNIFICATION OF GERMANY

Some historians trace the First World War as far back as 1815, when the French emperor Napoleon I was defeated at the Battle of Waterloo and Prussia, Austria, Russia and Britain met at the Congress of Vienna to discuss the future of Europe. The treaty of Vienna was designed to re-establish European stability by destroying Napoleon's Grand Empire and strengthening the power of hereditary rulers.

At this time Germany was made up of many independent states. The largest states, Austria and Prussia, competed for leadership of all the German-speaking peoples.

In 1862 Otto von Bismarck became Prussia's prime minister. Bismarck prepared for the unification of Germany in three short wars. In 1863 they defeated Denmark. Two years later, the Prussian army shattered the Austrians in a brilliant six-week campaign. Finally in 1870, to the amazement of neutral observers, the Prussians and their German allies overwhelmed France.

Prussia now dominated Germany and the smaller states looked to her for leadership. The German Empire was proclaimed in January 1871 with Prussia's King Wilhelm I as its emperor, or Kaiser. Otto von Bismarck became chancellor of united Germany. In May, France accepted a humiliating peace, paying hefty reparations and handing over the prosperous provinces of Alsace and Lorraine to the new German Empire.

BISMARCK'S ALLIANCES

The British were not unduly concerned by the formation of a German Empire. Having for centuries regarded France as their main adversary, they looked on Germany as a potential ally.

German unification had a far greater impact on continental Europe. France was anxious for revenge, in particular for the return of Alsace and Lorraine. Russia was suspicious of the new power on her western border. Bismarck realized that an alliance between France and Russia could spell disaster for Germany — it would be almost impossible for her to fight in the east and west at the same time. To prevent this happening, he determined to keep France isolated.

Bismarck's first step was to create the League of the Three Emperors (1872). This was a high-sounding but vague expression of friendship between the hereditary emperors of Germany, Russia and Austria-Hungary. More importantly, in 1879 Bismarck made the Dual Alliance with Austria-Hungary. The two empires agreed to help each other in a possible future conflict. Bismarck got Italy to join the Alliance in 1882, making it a Triple Alliance. He calmed Russian fears by renewing the League of the Three Emperors and drawing up a Reinsurance Treaty (1887), by which Germany and Russia promised not to go to war with one another.

As long as Bismarck guided German policy, France could only dream of revenge. Then, in 1888, Wilhelm II became Kaiser. Young and ambitious, he wanted Germany to be a major world power. By Christmas 1891 Bismarck's safety-first policy lay in ruins: the chancellor had resigned and Russia was looking about for a secure ally. At last, France had the chance she had been waiting for.

FRANCE AND RUSSIA

France and Russia were about as different as two countries could be. France was a republic and the home of modern European revolution. Russia, ruled by an autocratic Tsar, stood for conservatism and stability. Twice in the century the two powers had gone to war with each other. Nevertheless, by the 1890s things had changed sufficiently for them to set aside their suspicions and draw together.

The two nations did have some things in common. They were both jealous of Britain's colonial power. They were also worried lest the Dual Alliance between Germany and Austria-Hungary laid the foundations for a huge German-speaking empire, stretching from the Baltic to Baghdad. Nineteenth-century Russians saw themselves as protectors of fellow Slavs everywhere, including those in the Balkans. This policy, known as 'Panslavism', brought Russia into conflict with Austria-Hungary, which had many Slavs under its government.

The Russians and French began negotiations in 1891. By January 1894 they were officially linked in a Dual Alliance of their own. As well as sharing military plans, they forged strong economic links. French capital and technical know-how enabled Russia's infant industrial revolution to grow at a phenomenal rate. The bulk of the money for the Trans-Siberian railway, for example, came from France.

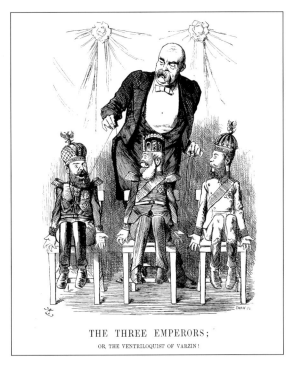

THE THREE EMPERORS;
OR, THE VENTRILOQUIST OF VARZIN!

This cartoon from the British magazine Punch, *shows the German chancellor Otto von Bismarck as a puppet master. He is skilfully controlling the emperors of Germany, Russia and Austria-Hungary, all members of his League of the Three Emperors.*

Without alliances, her [England's] fate will be ultimately pressed out between Russia and the United States. With my army and your fleet that combination against us will be powerless.

Kaiser Wilhelm II of Germany, suggesting an Anglo-German alliance in the 1890s.

TWO ARMED CAMPS

As the century drew to a close, continental Europe was divided into two armed camps: the Triple Alliance of Germany, Austria-Hungary and Italy, and the Dual Alliance of France and Russia. This alliance system created a balance of power that made the continent more stable than it had been for some time.

THE END OF BRITISH ISOLATION

If France is attacked by Germany, or by Italy supported by Germany, Russia shall employ all her available forces to attack Germany.
If Russia is attacked by Germany, or by Austria supported by Germany, France shall employ all her available forces to fight Germany.

From the military agreement that formed part of the Franco-Russian Alliance of 1893-4.

Britain, with no significant ally, was now the odd one out among the European powers. Until the very end of the century this did not matter much. Britain was the world's leading economic and industrial power, with a massive world-wide empire protected by a huge navy. What need had she to get tangled up with alliances? Conservative minister Lord Salisbury went so far as to describe his country's isolation as 'splendid'.

By the beginning of the new century, British isolation was looking more dangerous than splendid. Her worry was that imperial rivalry — which will be discussed fully in the next chapter — might provoke a full-scale European war. Confronted by either the Triple or Dual Alliance — or even a combination of the two — Britain would be seriously outnumbered. She needed an ally.

The first move, somewhat surprisingly, came from Japan. By the Anglo-Japanese Alliance of 1902 the two countries agreed to oppose Russian claims on Manchuria, in northern China. If war broke out, Japan would tackle Russian land forces while Britain kept France neutral.

Théophile Delcassé, the French foreign minister, was keen on his Dual Alliance with Russia, but it was primarily aimed at controlling Germany, not Britain. He had no wish to fight Britain to support Russia in the Far East. The obvious answer to his problem was to bring about a 'diplomatic revolution' and come to some sort of understanding with Britain.

He [King Edward VII] seemed to have captured Paris by storm. From that moment everything was changed wherever we went. Not only the King but all of the suite were received with loud and repeated cheering. It was the most marvellous transformation ....

Sir Frederick Ponsonby, who accompanied Edward VII on his state visit to France in 1903, reflecting on the success of a speech in which the king said that in Paris he felt as if he were at home.

The exchange of state visits between King Edward VII of Britain and President Loubet of France provoked a ground swell of public goodwill in 1903. When Russia and Japan went to war over Korea in 1904, Britain and France remained neutral. Two months later they signed their famous Entente Cordiale.

The Entente (understanding) settled long-running disputes over such places as Newfoundland and Nigeria. In return for recognizing British supremacy in Egypt, the French got Britain's secret acceptance that, if the government of the Sultan of Morocco collapsed, France might add his territory to their empire. Although it was a colonial agreement and not an alliance, the Entente soon led to Anglo-French military co-operation.

THE TRIPLE ENTENTE

The Anglo-French Entente was immediately tested when Kaiser Wilhelm II went to Tangier, Morocco, in 1905 to pledge German support for the country's independence. France was in a difficult position. She was not certain Britain would stand by her. Russia, her ally, had suffered a series of humiliating defeats at the hands of the Japanese. In addition, Russia's Tsar Nicholas II had been persuaded to enter into a defensive alliance with Germany.

By 1906, however, when the powers met in Spain to resolve the Moroccan problem, Germany's position had deteriorated. Tsar Nicholas II had abandoned the idea of a Russo-German alliance. In September 1905 US President Theodore Roosevelt had brokered peace between Japan and Russia (Portsmouth, New Hampshire). Britain, guided by officials who saw Germany as the greatest threat to British interests, stood by the Entente and backed France. In 1906, the Algeciras Conference, chaired by President Roosevelt, recognised Moroccan independence but left France in a strong position there.

Algeciras represented a serious setback for Germany. Worse was to follow. In August 1907 Russia and Britain agreed to settle their long-standing colonial differences in Afghanistan and Persia. This created a Triple Entente of Britain, France and Russia to match the Triple Alliance of Germany, Austria-Hungary and Italy.

Like the Anglo-French Entente, the Anglo-Russian Entente was a colonial agreement, not a military alliance. However, the members of the Triple Entente were all major powers, whereas Germany was the only major power in the Triple Alliance. As time went on, the Germans had an uneasy feeling that they were being encircled.

An agreement with Russia was the natural complement of the agreement with France; it was also the only practical alternative to the old policy of drift, with its continual complaints, bickerings, and dangerous friction.

Sir Edward Grey, British foreign secretary 1905-16.

Japanese warships destroy Russia's Baltic Fleet in the Straits of Tsushima, May 1905.

IMPERIAL AND COMMERCIAL RIVALRY

The alliances and ententes signed before the First World War are best understood as symptoms rather than causes of international rivalry. Significant tension was also created between nations by imperial and commercial competition. The two were closely linked. An empire, with its exclusive markets and sources of supply, was believed to bring huge commercial benefit to the mother country.

IMPERIAL RIVALRY

The period from about 1850 to 1914 is often called the 'Age of Imperialism', when the powers used their military, technological and commercial might to seize less developed parts of the world for their empires. An empire brought its possessor both prosperity and prestige. It was vital, therefore, for an imperialist nation to protect and, if possible, expand its overseas possessions. This invariably led to conflict between rival powers.

The British were by far the most successful imperialists. Their empire (on which, they declared proudly, 'the sun never sets') occupied one quarter of the world's land surface. It included India, Australia, New Zealand and Canada, bases such as Hong Kong and Aden, numerous far-flung islands and a huge swathe of African territory that ran in an almost unbroken line from Cape Town to Cairo.

Before the ententes with France (1904) and Russia (1907), these powers had posed the greatest threat to the British empire. On three occasions Britain sent military expeditions into Afghanistan to make sure that the country did not fall into Russian hands. In 1898 she prepared to fight France for the

MARCHEZ! MARCHAND!

GENERAL JOHN BULL (to MAJOR MARCHAND). "COME, PROFESSOR, YOU'VE HAD A NICE LITTLE SCIENTIFIC TRIP! I'VE SMASHED THE DERVISHES—LUCKILY FOR *YOU*—AND NOW I RECOMMEND YOU TO PACK UP YOUR FLAGS, AND GO HOME!!"

A cartoon from the time of the Anglo-French confrontation at Fashoda on the Upper Nile, 1898. When French forces under Major Marchand, advancing from the west, met the British forces of General Kitchener a colonial war looked possible. As this Punch *cartoon shows, the British were in no mood to withdraw.*

possession of the Sudan (the Fashoda Incident). By 1900, however, things were changing. A major reason why Britain settled her differences with France and Russia was that there was a new and aggressive player on the imperial board — Germany.

In the 1890s Kaiser Wilhelm II launched his country's *welt-politik*, or 'world scheme'. As if trying to make up for lost time, Germany set about taking what she called her 'place in the sun'. By the end of the century her colonies included Kiaochow (China), Western Samoa and three large tracts of southern and central Africa. The British regarded German imperialism as a direct threat to their own international position. They were further worried when the Germans announced a massive expansion of their navy, which will be discussed in the next chapter.

MEANWHILE, IN AMERICA

The formation of the German Empire had little immediate impact in the US, where the policy of successive administrations was to stay well clear of European affairs. They had more than enough on their hands back home, dealing with the effects of rapid industrialization and westward expansion.

During the 1890s, the US flexed its new-found muscle, too. By 1900, after a 'splendid little war' with Spain, the US occupied the Philippines, Guam, part of Samoa, Hawaii and Puerto Rico. Now proud possessor of a powerful navy, the US was regularly consulted on matters of international concern. This is why US President Theodore Roosevelt was called upon to mediate between Russia and Japan in 1905 and helped persuade the Kaiser to accept the Algeciras settlement of 1906.

Britain was the only European nation to befriend America during her war with Spain. The gesture was a sign of improving Anglo-US relations. Early in the new century Britain withdrew much of her military presence from the Caribbean, accepting that the region was now within the US sphere of influence. Britain's growing friendship with the US was crucial when war broke out in Europe in 1914.

... this powerful race [American Anglo-Saxons] will move down upon Mexico, down upon Central and South America, out upon the islands of the sea, over upon Africa and beyond.

The American Rev Joshiah Strong in his immensely popular imperialist manifesto *Our Country*, 1885.

COMMERCIAL RIVALRY

Commercial rivalry was important in building up international tension before the outbreak of European war in 1914. The First World War was not a commercial war, however. It was triggered by hostility between two states — Austria-Hungary and Serbia — whose commercial rivalry was minimal. Moreover, Anglo-US relations were improving at a time when economic competition between them was fiercer than ever.

Britain was the first country to experience an industrial revolution and by 1851 she was by far the world's greatest economic power. Fifty years later the situation was changing fast. The economies of all industrial nations had grown rapidly, but those of the US and Germany had made the most spectacular progress.

By 1900 only 35 per cent of the 76 million Americans still lived on farms. The US had more kilometres of railway than any other country. Her industrial output, which almost doubled between 1900 and 1914, was rapidly overtaking all competitors. When war broke out in 1914, the US was ideally suited to supply the combatants' needs. American goods had to be transported to Europe by ship and they were liable to be intercepted. America's economic position was going to make neutrality difficult to maintain.

German economic success was an even greater threat to Britain's position in the world. Between 1870 and 1914 coal production soared 800 per cent to rival Britain's. By the outbreak of war she was producing as much iron as Britain and twice as much steel. Her electricity output matched that of Britain, France and Italy combined, while her electrical and chemical industries led the world. Everywhere the British looked, they saw signs of Germany's new-found power. It was hardly a situation to promote harmony between the two peoples.

While French development did not match that of Germany, French capital enabled the Russian economy to advance at a phenomenal rate. Before long she had overtaken her ally in coal, iron and steel output. Given Russia's huge population (more than twice Germany's) and immense natural resources, there was a fair chance that within a couple of decades she would be challenging Germany for leadership of continental Europe. Glancing east, the Germans began to wonder whether a war sooner rather than later might not be the best way of tackling the Russian threat.

The mighty Krupp steel works at Essen, Germany in 1915. Following unification, German industry advanced at a pace that alarmed her rivals.

BACKGROUND TO WAR

THE ARMS RACE

Sir Edward Grey, the British Foreign Minister, argued that the alliance system encouraged an arms race. When one country increased its armed forces, its potential enemies had to do the same to keep up. In response, the first country built up its forces still further, and so on. Grey thought this military escalation — the arms race — 'made war inevitable'. Not all eventual combatants were caught up in the arms race. The US, for example, would have nothing to do with the arms build up. Congress voted for sufficient funds to maintain a powerful navy, but an army of about 300 thousand was considered quite sufficient to meet the country's needs. Even if the US had wanted to participate in the European war in 1914, she would have been in no position to do so effectively.

ARMIES

France recovered swiftly from the defeat by Prussia in 1870. She paid off the reparations to Germany ahead of schedule and went on to reorganize and strengthen her armed forces. Conscription was introduced for all men between the ages of 20 and 40, and for 20 years her army spending exceeded Germany's.

Confident that France alone could not defeat them, the Germans were not unduly concerned by the French recovery. What did worry them, however, was the Franco-Russian alliance of 1894. Now, as Bismarck had long feared, Germany faced the frightening prospect of having to fight on two fronts. The Russian army was 300 thousand men larger than Germany's in 1900. It was popularly viewed as a 'steamroller' — once it got going, it would crush everything in its path. Not surprisingly, the German generals built up their forces and prepared plans to fight France and Russia simultaneously.

Diplomatic crises led to further military escalation. After failing to get her way in Morocco in 1906, Germany put more trust in armed force than diplomacy. By 1914 there were some 4.5 million Germans with military training. Britain had less than a million men in her armies and reserves, and most were required for imperial duties. However, the Moroccan crisis led to the establishment of the British Expeditionary Force (BEF) of 150 thousand well-trained soldiers ready to cross the English Channel at short notice.

When Russia modernized her war plans after 1908, Austria-Hungary responded by enlarging her army and reserves to 3 million by 1914. In 1913 Russia moved one step further ahead by introducing a 'Great Military Programme' to increase her armed forces by ten per cent per annum. Within a year her regulars and reservists totalled almost 6 million men.

In terms of sheer manpower, Russia was bound to win any arms race. Add to this the rapid Russian industrial expansion we saw in the last chapter, and it is no surprise that by 1914 the German generals were worried. Their only hope of winning a war against the Triple Entente, they argued, lay in a massive pre-emptive strike.

NAVIES

The naval arms race was led by Britain. In the 1890s she adopted the Two Power Standard which said that the Royal Navy should be at least as large as any other

The way to make war impossible is to make victory certain.

Winston Churchill, future British Prime Minister, 1908.

Punch's *view of the Anglo-German naval race. The launching of HMS* Dreadnought *(1906) was intended to confirm Britain's naval supremacy by rendering all other warships obsolete. Instead, it fuelled the determination of her rivals to catch up.*

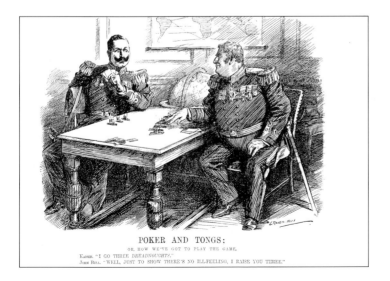

POKER AND TONGS;
OR, HOW WE'VE GOT TO PLAY THE GAME.
KAISER. "I GO THREE *DREADNOUGHTS.*"
JOHN BULL. "WELL, JUST TO SHOW THERE'S NO ILL-FEELING, I RAISE YOU THREE."

two fleets combined. At the time, these were assumed to be France and Russia. When either of them laid down new ships, Britain laid down an equal number.

The situation grew more complicated with the emergence of three new naval powers — Japan, the US and Germany. As the Japanese and Americans were friendly powers, their naval expansion caused Britain few worries. The US fleet continued to grow and in 1916 the Wilson administration launched a naval building programme to bring it up to parity with Britain. On the other hand, the build up of the German navy was more responsible than anything else for a serious deterioration in Anglo-German relations before 1914.

The original purpose of Germany's new navy was to put pressure on Britain to join the Triple Alliance. German Navy Laws of 1898 and 1900 planned the production of 38 new German battleships by 1920. Instead of drawing Britain into the alliance, the programme had

[We must] say to Germany ... the situation you have created is intolerable. If you determine to fight us, if you insist upon war, war you shall have; but the time shall be of our choosing and not of yours, and that time shall be now.

From an article in the British magazine *Nineteenth Century*, April 1910.

Talk of war. A French cartoon shows German Emperor William II as a sword-sharpening war-monger (1908). The heading Sommes-nous prêts ? *(Are We Ready?) warns the French to be prepared for war.*

the opposite effect. In the words of Winston Churchill, the future British prime minister, a large German fleet was 'a luxury'. Its only purpose, many argued, was to threaten British imperial and commercial interests.

Britain responded in 1906 by launching the turbine-driven British Dreadnought class of battleship, capable of sinking an entire fleet of less modern vessels single-handed. Germany replied with another Navy Law, laying down Dreadnoughts of her own and widening the Kiel Canal to accommodate them.

Despite an attempt in 1912 to reach a negotiated settlement, the cripplingly expensive naval arms race went on. By 1914 Britain boasted 57 major ships to her rival's 37 and irreparable damage had been done to Anglo-German relations. British naval power, once scattered world-wide, was now heavily concentrated in home waters. It was focused against a nation which, only 20 years earlier, had seemed her most likely European ally.

Germany must strive ... first to strike down one of the allies while the other is kept occupied; but then ... it must ... bring a superiority of numbers to the other theatre of war, which will also destroy the other enemy.

Count Alfred von Schlieffen, Chief of the German General Staff 1891-1905.

WAR PLANS

The nations of Europe not only built up their armed forces, they planned how to use them. Britain was ready to send the British Expeditionary force to France and to use her navy to blockade German ports. France was prepared to move into Alsace and Lorraine, while the Russians brought their might to bear on Germany's other flank. The German plans were the most original and the most dangerous.

In 1892 German Chief of Staff von Schlieffen pointed out that a major European war would probably involve Germany fighting against France in the west and Russia in the east. To cope with this, he proposed to knock out France with a swift advance on Paris, then transfer the bulk of the German armies east to face the Russians. As the technologically backward Russia would be slower to mobilize than France, the Schlieffen Plan made sound strategic sense.

The Plan's significance was two-fold. Firstly, it involved the German forces passing through Belgium, whose neutrality Britain had guaranteed. Secondly, unlike the war plans of the other major powers, it was aggressive. It required the Central Powers (Germany and Austria-Hungary) to strike first. Therefore, if a war between the Triple Alliance and the Triple Entente looked likely, there was a chance the Germans might strike first in order to give the Schlieffen Plan a chance to work.

THE TRIGGERS OF WAR 1908-1914

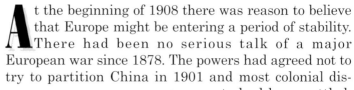

'But who will decide which way peace will go?' A German cartoon of 1908.

At the beginning of 1908 there was reason to believe that Europe might be entering a period of stability. There had been no serious talk of a major European war since 1878. The powers had agreed not to try to partition China in 1901 and most colonial disagreements had been settled. Neither of the major non-European powers, Japan and the USA, had any interest in disturbing European stability.

But as we have seen, all was not calm below the surface. The precarious balance of power maintained through a network of alliances and ententes was threatened by colonial, commercial and military rivalry. Governments and their military advisors talked of war and planned for it. There was peace, not because the alternative was unthinkable, but because no crisis had yet come along that was serious enough to merit war.

CRISIS AFTER CRISIS

The short-lived calm ended in the Balkans, the volatile region of fierce loyalties sometimes called the 'Powder Keg of Europe'. In 1897 and 1903 Russia and Austria-Hungary, the region's rival masters, had agreed to co-operate to maintain peace. The agreement collapsed in 1908 when Austria-Hungary formally annexed the largely Serb provinces of Bosnia and Herzegovina, which it had administered since 1878.

The furious Russian government regarded Austria-Hungary's action as unmerited Germanic

Guerrillas in the Balkan state of Macedonia plan the next move against their Turkish overlords. The weakness of Turkish power in the Balkans was a major cause of the region's mounting instability.

interference with Slav peoples. Germany stood by her alliance with Austria-Hungary. Russia's friends, on the other hand, did not think the situation serious enough for military action. Russia could not act without French or British support, so she backed down. Great power agreement over the Balkans was finished.

In 1911 the focus of international attention shifted back to Morocco. When French troops broke the agreement made at the Algeciras Conference in 1906, Germany sent the gunboat *Panther* to the Moroccan port of Agadir, Britain put her fleet on alert and France cancelled military leave. For a time it looked as if the crisis might flare into war. A peaceful settlement was eventually worked out by which Germany got land in the Congo in return for recognizing French supremacy in Morocco. The Kaiser was not pleased.

Germany had now given way twice over Morocco (1906 and 1911). Russia had given way over

The Bosnia-Herzegovina crisis revealed with unmistakable clearness the aims of Austro-German policy in the Balkans and laid the foundation for an inevitable conflict between Germanism and Slavism.

From the memoirs of Russian Foreign Minister Serge Sazonov.

Bosnia-Herzegovina (1908). Neither power would be prepared to face further humiliation.

By 1912 Macedonia was one of the few Balkan territories still under Turkish rule — but not for long. The Russians, eager to show that they still counted for something in the region, persuaded Serbia and Bulgaria to join forces against Macedonia. Greece and Montenegro joined in, the Turks were crushed and a peace patched together in London (May 1913).

Almost immediately Serbia and Bulgaria fell out over who got what. A second Balkan war broke out in which Serbia, Greece, Romania and Turkey crushed Bulgaria. In the peace treaty that marked the end of the Balkan Wars, Serbia gained considerably, much to the irritation of Austria-Hungary.

The triumph of Russian-backed Panslavism during the Balkan Wars had two effects. First,

Serbian women receive military training, 1908. The growing military might of Russian-backed Serbia was of great concern to neighbouring Austria-Hungary.

Germany drew closer to the Ottoman Turks, whom she needed as an ally against further Slav expansion. Secondly, Austria-Hungary became obsessed by the threat posed by Serbia. By the beginning of 1914 the government in Vienna was determined to end the danger on its southern frontier once and for all. The assassination of Archduke Franz Ferdinand gave it just the excuse it needed.

THE GAMBLE

Austria-Hungary's decision to crush Serbia was not a reckless gamble. Serbia would obviously look to Russia for support, but Russia was unlikely to act without Britain and France. As they had not previously shown much support for Russia's Balkan ambitions, there was little reason to suppose that these two countries would act differently in 1914. It was likely, therefore, that Russia would complain but stop short of war, as in 1908.

Moreover, the assassination, for which Serbia was generally believed to be responsible, was greeted with widespread international revulsion. No crowned head, least of all the Tsar of Russia (whose grandfather had been killed by an anarchist bomb), wanted to be seen as a supporter of terrorism. If Austria-Hungary acted swiftly and decisively, she would have international opinion on her side. It all depended on how quickly she could react.

The first response came fast. On 5 July, a week after the assassination, the Kaiser gave Austria-Hungary a 'blank cheque' of support for the elimination of Serbia. This timely show of support for Germany's principal ally was in keeping with Germany's own desire to prop up the Ottoman Empire as a barrier against Slav expansion.

THE ULTIMATUM

If the government in Vienna had cashed the Kaiser's 'blank cheque' immediately and attacked Serbia, the crisis might not have spread. But the Austrians and Hungarians could not agree what to do. The Austrians wanted to strike hard and fast. The Hungarians called for a more restrained response. Weeks slipped by. Russia's resolve to stand by Serbia hardened.

The Royal Serbian Government will ... pledge itself to ... remove from military service and from the administration all officers and officials who are guilty of having taken part in the propaganda against Austria-Hungary, whose names ... the Imperial and Royal Government [of Austro-Hungary] will communicate.

From the ultimatum presented to Serbia by the government of Austria-Hungary, July 1914.

The Kaiser authorized me to inform our gracious Majesty that we might in this case, as in all others, rely upon Germany's full support ....

The Austrian ambassador in Berlin tells the Austro-Hungarian foreign minister of Wilhelm II's 'blank cheque' of support for action against Serbia, July 1914.

Finally, on 23 July, Austria-Hungary sent her ultimatum to Serbia. To avoid invasion, she had to accept every clause.

If Serbia had accepted the ultimatum, she would have become an Austro-Hungarian satellite. Russia's influence among the Balkan Slavs was at stake, so she assured Serbia of her support. The Tsar was not seeking war, but he had been backed into a corner and this time France stood by him. The only way out of the crisis was for Austria-Hungary to climb down — something the Kaiser urged her not to do.

To most people's surprise, Serbia accepted most clauses of the ultimatum. Even that, however, was not enough. On 28 July 1914, Austria-Hungary declared war on Serbia.

STEP BY STEP TOWARDS WAR

The 'steamroller' in action: Russian forces parade before Tsar Nicholas II in 1914. The mighty Russian army, so feared before the war, proved no match for the better led and equipped Germans.

The Russians ordered a full mobilization of their forces (something very difficult to reverse), but did not declare war. The final, irretrievable step was taken by Germany. She sent an ultimatum to Russia on 31 July and declared war the following day. The Schlieffen Plan swung into operation. On 2 August German troops entered Luxembourg. War with France came on 3 August and with Britain a day later.

NATIONALISM AND OTHER LONG-TERM CAUSES OF WAR

In the final analysis, three long-term factors were of primary importance in the run up to the war of 1914. The first was the failure of other nations to accommodate Germany as the dominant power in continental Europe. The second was the inability of Austria-Hungary and Russia to sort out peacefully their differences over the Balkans. The third was nationalism.

Nationalism, or loyalty for one's own country, was an obsession in Europe. Politicians used it, entertainers sang of it, journalists exalted it. It inspired men and women from Athens to London to believe that it was a truly noble thing *pro patria mori*: to die for one's country. The sentiment was perhaps strongest in the newest countries, notably Germany and Serbia, and among the ruling classes. In America, with its multi-national society, nationalism was less apparent.

Europe's ruling elite had much in common. Most had been educated in a rather old-fashioned code, loosely based on the virtues of ancient classical civilizations. These laid heavy stress on honour, duty and stoic resistance, whatever the odds. War, even death, was preferable to dishonour. What made such a philosophy tragically dangerous was that few of the great powers' generals or leading politicians had any first-hand experience of full-scale war. And no one, not even the military experts, had any idea of the terrible, long drawn out carnage of twentieth-century technological warfare. When they went to war, they did not know — quite literally — what they were letting themselves in for.

European rulers, even in such autocratic states as Russia, could not have risked war without a strong ground swell of popular support. Nationalism provided

TO THE YOUNG WOMEN OF LONDON

Is your "Best Boy" wearing Khaki? If not don't **YOU** **THINK** he should be?

If he does not think that you and your country are worth fighting for—do you think he is **WORTHY** of you?

Don't pity the girl who is alone—her young man is probably a soldier—fighting for her and her country—and for **YOU.**

If your young man neglects his duty to his King and Country, the time may come when he will **NEGLECT YOU.**

Think it over—then ask him to

JOIN THE ARMY TO-DAY

Emotional blackmail was just one of the tactics used to attract young men into Britain's volunteer army.

In ... [the Chief of the German General Staff, General von Moltke's] opinion there was no alternative to making a preventative war in order to defeat the enemy while we still had a chance of victory .... [He] therefore proposed that I should conduct a policy with the aim of provoking a war in the near future.

Gottlieb von Jagow, German Secretary of State for Foreign Affairs, 1913-16.

this. The alliance and entente systems ensured that the enemy were clearly defined. Commercial, imperial and military rivalry reinforced popular prejudice.

Because war was thought noble — even romantic — it was widely talked about. In 1908 the Austrian press had declared, 'Never was a war more just. And never yet was our confidence in a victorious outcome more firmly grounded.' Over the years that followed, the feeling grew that war was 'inevitable'. In France and Germany the military tended to the opinion that as war was bound to come, there was no point in trying too hard to avoid it.

L'INGORDO
TROP DUR

'The glutton trying to eat the world.' An Italian cartoon reinforcing popular prejudice by spreading the message that Kaiser William II aimed at global domination.

Devotion to one's country — right or wrong — made public humiliation hard to bear. Between 1906 and 1913 all the great European powers (with the possible exception of Britain) believed they had backed down for the sake of peace. Each successive retreat made a similar step more difficult in the future.

WHY 1914?

The crisis of 1914 was different from those that had preceded it: Germany had decided — rightly or wrongly — that an all-out European war was inevitable and the longer it was delayed, the less chance she had of victory. Hence, the 'blank cheque' to Austria-Hungary. The Schlieffen Plan ensured that Russia, France and, almost certainly, Britain would be drawn into the fighting.

Germany was not motivated by a simple desire for continental domination. As Allied military might was growing at a rate Germany could not match, she had a very real fear of encirclement and eventual dismemberment by her enemies. The German Empire had been founded only in 1871 and 43 years of existence was no guarantee of permanence.

In the July crisis both Austria-Hungary and Russia felt they could not give way. Had Vienna done so, her Balkan policy would have collapsed and Slav nationalism might have threatened the very existence of the Austro-Hungarian Empire. Had Russia backed down, she would have abandoned her fellow Slavs to a possible extension of Germanic power from Berlin to Baghdad. Too much was at stake to contemplate withdrawal, so Europe lurched into war.

In the United States, European problems still seemed very far away. Most Americans believed that their country was too isolated to become involved in the European war. They were reassured when, on 19 August 1914, President Wilson voiced the country's official stance regarding the war in the following words: 'The United States must be neutral in fact as well as in name during these days that are to try men's souls.'

At this stage most Americans failed to recognize that their national prosperity relied on international trade. It was inevitable that Europe's problems would have an impact on American industry.

THE WAR SPREADS

EUROPE, ASIA AND AFRICA

The war that began in July-August 1914 was not a world war. For a long time the conflict was known as the 'European War' or even the 'Great War'. The phrase 'World War' became common later, when the entry of the USA turned it into a genuinely global conflict.

STALEMATE AND SLAUGHTER

I, a single human being with my little stock of earthly experience in my head, was entering ... the veritable gloom and disaster of the thing called Armageddon. And I saw it then, as I see it now — a dreadful place, a place of horror and desolation which no imagination could have invented.

Siegfried Sassoon, a British infantry officer, on entering a front line trench.

The Schlieffen Plan failed. German troops rushed towards Paris through Luxembourg, Belgium and northern France but were stopped just short of the capital by the French army and the British Expeditionary Force. Over the following weeks the German and Allied armies spread out east and west in an attempt to outflank each other. By Christmas 1914 they were dug in along a front extending from Switzerland to the English Channel. And that, with a few minor variations, was where the Western Front remained for the next three-and-a-half years.

There was a bit more mobility in the east, where in 1914 the Germans defeated the Russians at Tannenberg and the Masurian Lakes and drove east across Poland. Further south, the Russians and Austro-Hungarians slogged it out in bloody campaigns at the foot of the Carpathian Mountains. By 1917 the Central Powers had advanced to a line running north-south from the Gulf of Riga to the Romanian border.

There were long periods of stalemate on both the Eastern and Western Fronts. This was because the tactics of defence — based around trenches, machine guns, barbed wire and artillery bombardments — were superior to the tactics of attack. The offensives, notably the German attack on Verdun and the British attempt to advance along the River Somme (both 1916), resulted in huge casualties and very little

territorial gain. For most of the war millions of men on both sides were subjected to the dreadful slaughter of trench warfare.

An Allied attempt to break the stalemate by landing troops on the Dardanelles, at the entrance to the Black Sea, ended in disaster (1915). There was scarcely any more action in the war at sea. The minor battles in 1914 and 1915 involved few ships. The only time the German High Seas fleet tried to leave port, May-June 1916, it inflicted heavy casualties on the British at Jutland but was forced to flee back to the safety of its minefields. After that, the Germans concentrated on submarine warfare while the Allies tried to bring the Central Powers to their knees by maintaining a close blockade of their ports.

Going 'over the top'. British troops begin an assault in the Battle of the Somme, 1916. The officers who led such futile attacks were invariably the first casualties.

THE SEARCH FOR ALLIES: EUROPE

As soon as the war broke out, both sides began to search frantically for allies. The prime catch, of course, would have been the US, but virtually all shades of American opinion were still against becoming involved in a bloody conflict thousands of kilometres away.

The first power to join the conflict was the Ottoman Empire, which aligned herself with the Central Powers at the end of October, 1914. This immediately widened the war zone to include most of the Middle East, where there was a British-backed Arab revolt against the Turks.

Italy, fearful of the damage an Anglo-French fleet might inflict on her vulnerable coastline, opted out of her commitment to the Triple Alliance. She then offered to support the Allies in return for a promise of all territory populated by Italian-speakers and part of the Adriatic coast claimed by Serbia. The Allies accepted these terms at the Treaty of London (May 1915) and Italy entered the war on their side.

The decision rebounded heavily on the Italians. They suffered a disastrous defeat at the hands of Austria-Hungary (Caporetto, 1917) and only partially redeemed the situation at Vittoria Veneto the following year.

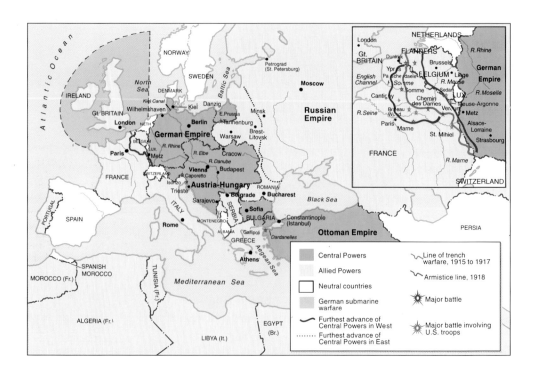

Bulgaria, humiliated during the Second Balkan War, was tempted to side with Serbia's enemies. However, she delayed committing herself to the Central Powers until 1915, when things were going badly for Russia and Serbia. She was eventually defeated by an Allied offensive around Salonika (September 1918). Romania joined the Allies in 1916, was defeated but rejoined the war to be included among the victors. Greece sided with the Allies in 1917, and by the cessation of hostilities in 1918 a further 11 countries, including Portugal and Brazil, had joined the same cause.

THE SEARCH FOR ALLIES: JAPAN AND THE EMPIRES

Shortly after the outbreak of the European War, Britain asked Japan to enter the conflict on her side. Japan willingly agreed and, to the consternation of the US and Australia, soon went beyond the minor role Britain had envisaged for her. She seized Germany's Asian colonies and early in 1915 presented China with Twenty-One Demands. If accepted, these would have reduced China to the status of a Japanese protectorate. When Britain and the US objected strongly, Japan dropped her most aggressive demands. She was left with claims on southern Manchuria that formed the springboard for further expansion later in the century. By 1919 the Japanese navy, undamaged by the fighting, was the third largest in the world.

Many recent immigrants to the US returned home to fight for the land of their birth. Soldiers from all over the British and French Empires were shipped to fight in Europe. Together with the world-wide naval conflict, this meant that the impact of the war was felt in the remote villages of North Africa and India, as well as the towns and farms of Australia, New Zealand, Canada and South Africa. The African mainland saw hard-fought campaigns, too. By November 1918, British imperial troops had overrun German East Africa. South African forces took German South-West Africa (1914-1915), an Anglo-Nigerian army occupied Cameroon (1915-1916) and an Anglo-French army took Togo in 1914. In effect, Germany had now disappeared from Africa as a colonial power.

The best prospects of India are linked up with the permanence of British rule. We desire to proclaim to the Kaiser and the enemies of England that behind the British Army is the whole of the Indian people ....

Indian nationalist leader Surendranath Banerjee, 1914. His remarks were widely used in Britain for propaganda purposes.

ENTER THE USA

THE US AS A WORLD POWER

With the 'splendid little war' against Spain in 1898, the US entered the ranks of the world powers. It was not a position that the country found easy to accept. On the one hand, American idealists condemned the way the powers used their might to interfere in the affairs of lesser nations. They wanted a new-style world diplomacy, based on openness and honesty, not military alliances and a dangerous 'balance of power.' On the other hand, US economic interests, particularly in the Caribbean and Central America, made it impossible for her not to take an active interest in the domestic politics of her neighbours.

In 1905 President Theodore Roosevelt announced his famous corollary to the Monroe Doctrine. In cases of 'chronic wrong-doing', he declared, the US reserved the right to intervene in countries within its sphere of influence. 'Chronic wrong-doing' meant, essentially, acting contrary to the wishes of US businessmen and politicians. The US had already annexed Puerto Rico (1898), made Panama a protectorate (1903) and occupied Cuba (1898-1902). By the end of 1916 she had re-occupied Cuba and occupied Nicaragua, Vera Cruz (Mexico), Haiti and the Dominican Republic. In other words, although Americans might talk of guiding the world towards 'justice, liberty and peace', self-interest obliged their leaders — even theoretical peacemakers such as President Woodrow Wilson — to act otherwise.

The US's more positive role in world affairs had already brought her up against

Theodore ('Teddy') Roosevelt (1858-1919). Defeated by Woodrow Wilson in the 1912 presidential race, he then campaigned strongly for the US to enter the war on the Allied side.

Germany. Intervention in Venezuela (1903) and Dominica (1905) had thwarted German policy. At the 1906 Algeciras Conference, President Roosevelt had sided against the Kaiser. Nevertheless, as we know, when Europe went to war in 1914, it was the president's intention to be 'impartial in thought as well as deed'. The corrupt Old World could blow itself to pieces if it wished, but that was not the concern of the New. It remained to be seen how realistic this attitude was.

President Wilson's women's campaign auto, 1916. Note the second point of the manifesto — less than a year after this picture was taken Congress declared war on Germany.

AMERICA GOES TO WAR

The US was too powerful to be tempted by the promise of territory if she joined either the Allies or the Central Powers. Besides, in 1912 the electorate had chosen as president a liberal, progressive Democrat, Woodrow Wilson, who was determined to keep the US out of the European war.

From the outset, however, key sections of US society strongly favoured the Allied cause. The president himself was an avowed Anglophile. The East Coast establishment, with its powerful cultural, racial and emotional links with the Anglo-Saxon world, was strongly sympathetic towards the democratic governments of Britain and France. Germanic militarism was an anathema to them. The bulk of the more influential press favoured the Allied cause.

US propaganda, 1917. A fresh-faced American takes up the standard to lead his tired European allies against the 'barbarous Hun'.

My dream is that as the years go on and the world knows more of America, it ... will turn to America for those moral inspirations which lie as the basis of all freedoms ....

Woodrow Wilson addressing a Fourth of July audience, 1914.

In the great cities, particularly among the Irish and those with left-wing views, the Allied cause was less popular. Germany, after all, had adopted a form of state socialism and Russian autocracy was about as far as one could get from the American ideal of government.

From 1914-1916 Wilson made several unsuccessful attempts to mediate between the two sides. Politically his continued neutrality was popular and he won the 1916 election under the slogan 'He Kept Us Out of the War'. By late 1916, however, American neutrality was wearing thin. Four factors accounted for this.

Firstly, Britain won the propaganda war. American journalists based in Britain wrote up the Allied cause and depicted the Germans as 'barbarians'. By 1915 even presidential advisors were suggesting that, for the sake of civilization, 'Germany must not be allowed to win the war'.

Secondly, the actions of some of the belligerents directly affected US interests overseas. The most obvious example was Japan's proposed advance into China. Anglo-American co-operation to thwart Japanese plans served to remind the two Atlantic powers of their common interests. This tied in with a feeling in US military circles that the neutrality of the North Atlantic could be guaranteed only by a British victory in Europe.

Thirdly, the outbreak of war led to an immediate demand for American goods of every kind, particularly food and armaments, giving the US economy a timely boost. Before 1914 the bulk of US transatlantic trade had been with Britain. The war accentuated this trend, helped by the British blockade of Germany and a US government declaration that trade with the Allies was 'legal and welcome'. By 1916 Allied trade with the US had risen by 400 per cent. American financiers also invested millions of dollars in the Allied countries and put up $ 2.2 billion in loans. A German victory would spell economic disaster for the US.

Fourthly, the naval war impinged most directly on American neutrality. Both sides sought to hamper their enemies' war efforts by means of naval blockades. The difference lay in the methods they adopted. The British ignored US neutrality and mined the North Sea (informing neutral shipping of the danger) and used surface ships to intercept all vessels trading with the enemy. In the great majority of cases this did not involve loss of life.

Germany, whose High Seas Fleet was bottled up in harbour for almost the entire war, had to rely on submarine warfare. At first this was similar to a conventional blockade. U-boats surfaced near their targets, told the crews to take to the life boats, then sank their ships with gunfire or a single torpedo. But on the surface submarines were extremely vulnerable and in February 1915 Germany switched to unrestricted submarine warfare. All vessels suspected of trading with the Allies were liable to be sunk without warning.

'Forward the U-boats!' A German poster of 1917 reflects the country's hope that her 120 submarines would bring the Allies to their knees before US might could influence the outcome of the war in Europe.

The torpedoing of the unarmed British liner Lusitania *in May 1915, in which 128 Americans died, played an important part in swinging US public opinion against Germany.*

The most significant victim was the British liner *Lusitania*. On 7 May 1915 she was torpedoed off the Irish coast with a loss of 1,153 lives, including 128 Americans. Germany formally ended unlimited submarine warfare four months after the sinking of the *Luisitania* but in the US there were widespread calls for war with Germany. Pacifist Secretary of State William Jennings Bryan (the 'Prince of Peace') resigned in protest, convinced that his country was stepping ever nearer to war.

Two incidents finally pushed the US into war. The first was the reintroduction of Germany's 'sink at sight' submarine tactic on 1 February 1917. The second was the Zimmerman Telegram. German Foreign Minister Arthur Zimmerman sent a coded message on a privileged line put at his disposal by the US State Department (19 January 1917). The intended recipient was a German diplomat in Mexico. The telegram suggested that if Mexico joined the Central Powers, she would be rewarded with territory in the southern USA. It was also hinted that Japan might be induced to attack US bases in the Pacific.

British intelligence intercepted the telegram and passed its contents to the US administration. The American press were let in on the secret on 2 March. The clamour for a positive response was irrepressible and on 6 April 1917 Congress formally declared war on Germany. After more than two-and-a-half years of fighting, the Great War was now the World War.

THE USA AT WAR

The US entered the war with great enthusiasm. Patriotic groups, such as the American Defense Society, sprang up all over the country. Strikers, pacifists and other 'undesirables' were persecuted and unwanted aliens deported. The war, progressives felt, would 'purify' the nation, binding it together in a 'true national collectivism.'

To make the most of her resources, and to maintain a 'bridge of ships' to Europe, the US needed to co-ordinate and focus her efforts. To this end, the Council of National Defense was shaken up, greatly increasing the powers of the president and his staff. Other bodies, such as the War Industries Board and the Fuel Administration, were established to direct private enterprise. Young men were drafted into the armed forces. Business profits soared. Wages rose, too, but hardly kept pace with the cost of living, which doubled between 1913 and 1918. The workforce was dissatisfied and this lead to the creation of a National War Labour Board to mediate in disputes.

Thanks partly to these measures, the US played an important part in bringing the war to a swift and victorious end. But she was hardly 'purified' by the experience. Ordinary people were suspicious of the

Once lead this people into war, and they'll forget there ever was such a thing as tolerance. To fight you must be brutal and ruthless, and the spirit of ruthless brutality will enter into every fibre of our national life ....

President Woodrow Wilson on the eve of his speech to Congress calling for a declaration of war on Germany, April 1917.

President Wilson calls on Congress to declare war on Germany, on 3 April 1917. Three days later Congress complied with the president's wishes. With US involvement, the Great European War became a World War.

41

Total war. Americans soon learned that war involved more than just sending troops overseas — every aspect of life, even eating habits, was affected by the drive for victory.

unprecedented increase in federal power and irritated at the scale of the profits made by the few. By 1918 the majority of Americans were looking forward to peace.

VICTORY

We have no selfish ends to serve. We desire no conquest, no dominion. We seek no indemnities ... no material compensation .... The world must be made safe for democracy.

President Woodrow Wilson, 6 April 1917.

From the Allied point of view, the US entered the war just in time. France had fought herself to a standstill. Britain, reeling from the shock of losing virtually an entire generation of young men, was desperately short of both soldiers and munitions. Worse still, the Tsar's government had been overthrown by revolution in March 1917. Although the new, professedly democratic government fought on, the Russian people had reached the limit of their tolerance. The Communists seized power in November, promising 'Peace, Bread, Land'. Peace came to Russia with the harsh Treaty of Brest-Litovsk (March, 1918), by which Russia surrendered vast tracts of productive land to the Central Powers.

Although things were tough in Britain and France, they were perhaps even worse in Germany and Austria-Hungary. The war-weary German population was starving. The government of Austria-Hungary managed to continue fighting only by declaring martial law. With the arrival of the first US troops in January 1918, the Central Powers knew that if they failed on the Western Front that spring, all would be lost.

Reinforced by the US contingent that would eventually number 2 million men, the Allies fought off the 1918 German Spring Offensive. That summer it was their turn to attack. Tanks and aircraft finally broke the deadlock of trench warfare and the Germans began to retreat, suffering gigantic losses. On 3 November Austria-Hungary collapsed and the German fleet mutinied. Two days later the guns on the Western Front finally fell silent.

American troops landing at Southampton, England. Although it took almost a year for US strength to have an impact on the course of the war, the 1 million men they had in the field by November 1917 proved decisive in bringing about Germany's defeat.

THE COST OF WAR

In formal terms the First World War ended on 11 November 1918, when an armistice came into effect on the Western Front. While it was still in progress, it was clear that the war was the most murderous, destructive conflict the world had ever seen. Just as it had no neat beginning, it came to no neat close. In some areas the fighting had already stopped, in others it went on into the following year. Though Russia had made peace in 1918, the international war merged with a civil war that lasted for another five dreadful years. By keeping a blockade on German ports until July 1919, the Allies went on killing men, women and children through starvation and deprivation long after the last shots had been fired on the battlefields.

Such high hopes! The victorious Allies celebrate the end of the war in November 1918.

THE HUMAN COST

In all combatant countries some 70 million men were called up into the armed forces. Of these, about 9 million (13 per cent) died. The Germans lost over 2 million,

the French about 1.4 million and the British Empire almost 1 million. The enormous Russian figures cannot be accurately estimated, although they were probably slightly less than those of Germany.

The percentage figures are yet more telling. Serbia lost 37 per cent of its fighting forces, Turkey 27 per cent Romania, 26 per cent and Bulgaria 22 per cent. The major powers lost comparatively fewer: France 17 per cent, Germany 16 per cent, Austria-Hungary and Britain about 12.5 per cent (less than Australia and New Zealand) and Russia 12 per cent. About 116 thousand US soldiers were killed, some 4 per cent of those under arms.

Casualties exceeded deaths several times over. Almost a quarter of a million British men, for example, lost an arm or a leg. 'Shell shock' — nervous collapse through the strain of constant fighting, all too often categorized as cowardice — ruined millions of lives. If we include deaths from the 'flu epidemic that ravaged the exhausted populations of post-war Europe, the number of civilian casualties exceeded those of combatants. Add to these figures the countless widows and orphans, the shattered dreams, the untold pain, misery and suffering, and we begin to get some idea why, when it was all over, men and women hoped and prayed that this had been 'the war to end all war'.

If we look at the losses more closely, it becomes clear why the survivors spoke of a 'lost generation'. To begin with, the early twentieth-century world was still accustomed to male leadership. The loss of so many

A British field dressing station behind the front lines at the Somme, 1916. By the end of the battle, which destroyed Britain's volunteer army, the overstretched emergency services had treated almost 400 thousand casualties.

men, therefore, took away a large proportion of society's traditional leaders. This was exaggerated by the fact that the casualty rate among officers (particularly junior officers, who were first 'over the top' in a trench attack) was higher than for ordinary soldiers. A country's officer class were the leaders of tomorrow, and by 1918 there were precious few of them left. Winston Churchill described Britain's post-war government as a 'government of the Second XI'.

THE POLITICAL COST

A French waiter presents the Kaiser with 'the bill' of over 1 million casualties suffered by both sides during the Battle of Verdun, 1916. Such horrendous losses made it almost inevitable that France's post-war leaders would impose the harshest possible peace terms on Germany.

The First World War was a total war. In their quest for victory, the governments of the warring countries took control of all available resources, human and well as material. For the duration of the war, the state was supreme — to question the government was at best unpatriotic, at worst an act of treason. Taxes rose, labour was directed, men conscripted into the armed forces, travel restricted, goods rationed. Governments of all descriptions employed the new and insidious weapon of propaganda to get their messages across. Men, women and children become used as never before to having their lives directed by higher authorities.

The massive accumulation of control into the hands of the central government did not wither away once the war was over. Even in the US, where central direction of the economy was dismantled quicker and more completely than elsewhere, the experience of the war was not totally erased. Nineteenth-century liberalism, with its emphasis on individual responsibility was gone for ever. The power of the state over its citizens remains the chief political legacy of the war.

War increased people's suspicions of minority groups. All outsiders were a potential danger. This feeling persisted after the war, particularly with regard to the Jews. The Jews had always been subject to

THE BILL

occasional but violent persecution, especially in Central and Eastern Europe. German and Austrian nationalists, looking for a racial scapegoat for their defeat, identified the Jews as an obvious target. Their prejudices were reinforced by the comments of the anti-Communists fleeing the Russian Civil War. The Russian Revolution, they declared, was part of a world-wide Jewish conspiracy.

The most vulnerable minority in the Ottoman Empire were the Armenians. During the war, almost half a million of them were massacred by the Turks. This act of terrible genocide later attracted the attention of the Nazis, sowing the seeds for the horrific events of the Holocaust.

Anti-Semitism, the bitter by-product of war. A French cartoon of 1916 attacks the Jews as sleek profiteers of the armaments industry. There were similar anti-Semitic outbursts in Germany and elsewhere in Eastern Europe.

THE ECONOMIC COST

In 1918 the agreed aim of Western politicians and industrialists was a return to normal life. It was an impossible target. The world economy had been turned on its head and the delicate pre-war balance broken for ever.

The United States emerged as the world's leading economic power. She largely financed the war and benefited hugely from the profits made before she joined. During the 1920s, despite trouble in the agricultural sector, US industrial output and average incomes rose steadily.

Britain's leadership of the world economy was gone for ever. She was saddled with huge debts and a brief post-war boom was followed by years of static exports, high unemployment and comparatively slow growth. Looking to the past for reassurance, governments unwisely tried to bring back the pre-war world of free trade and a pound stirling backed by gold reserves. France, too, suffered. Most of the loans she had made to Tsarist Russia were never repaid. Large

Do we wish to restore Germany to freedom and power? If 'yes', then the first thing to do is to rescue it from the Jew who is ruining our country.

Adolf Hitler, 1924.

47

The population here [in Poland] was living upon roots, grass, acorns and heather .... The distribution of food in the towns was very unequal. It was possible to buy almost anything in the restaurants at a price ... but in other parts of the same town it was impossible to buy any food.

A British relief director, 1919.

Hell on earth — the unreal landscape of the Somme valley after ceaseless bombardment by heavy artillery. Eighty years later, unexploded shells remain a danger in the 1914-1918 war zones.

areas in the east of the country were in ruins. To make matters worse, inflation hampered her efforts to meet the cost of reconstruction.

Germany's problems were even greater. Political instability, inflation, unemployment and the massive payments demanded by the Allies meant misery for millions throughout the 1920s.

In 1918 Russian industrial output was only 12 percent of its 1913 level. It recovered rapidly in the 1920s, but by then the country was virtually cut off from the world economy. Japan, whose prosperity had leaped during the war, found imports outstripping exports for much of the 1920s. Throughout the rest of the world, industrial and pre-industrial countries suffered similar problems to those of the technologically more advanced nations.

Instability was the war's key economic legacy. All countries faced periods of boom and recession, though these did not necessarily affect all countries at the same time. Inflation hampered trade. The demands of social welfare, reconstruction and replacing out-dated machinery often exceeded the money available. Good times fed hopes that could not be met in the long run. International co-operation to deal with these problems ('bankers' diplomacy') was piecemeal and short-term.

Nevertheless, by 1927 there were signs that the world economy was finally settling down. German manufacturing output exceeded the 1913 level for the first time since the war. That of the US was almost 50 per cent higher. But the foundations for recovery were both narrow and shallow. It took only a shudder from the US to bring the entire fabric of post-war prosperity tumbling down.

NEW WAR

The First World War brought a new era of warfare. In the long run the most significant development was air power, which brought civilians as well as soldiers into the firing line. The first to suffer were the people of Antwerp, in Belgium, who endured a zeppelin bombing raid on 25 August 1915. By 1918 planes such as the four-engined Handley Page 0/1500, a forerunner of the mighty bombers of the Second World War, were capable of reaching Berlin with up to 20 bombs, each weighing 113 kg. The rapid advance in aircraft technology paved the way for the growth of the civil aviation industry after the war. The aircraft was recognized by the formation of air forces as independent branches of the armed forces. The British Royal Air Force and the United States (Army) Air Service were both founded in 1918.

There were no advances of similar significance in naval warfare. The key roles of the battleship and the submarine were confirmed. One lasting development was the use of the convoy system for shepherding vulnerable cargo vessels across wide expanses of ocean. In another move of future importance, the British ordered the first purpose-built aircraft carrier, the *Argus*, in 1916.

Before 1917 the fighting on land proved what far-sighted commentators had suggested before the outbreak of war — that barbed wire and the machine gun would always give defenders the edge over attackers. By 1918 the days of cavalry as a realistic fighting force in all but small-scale operations were over. The use of poisonous gas, the cause of terrible suffering during the First World War, foreshadowed modern chemical and germ warfare.

The major lesson of the land battles for future conflicts was learned only towards the end of the war. The deployment of tanks, first used successfully at Cambrai in 1917, heralded a new era of offensive

The news continues to be good, the tanks seem to have done good work and fairly put the wind up the Hun, who was seen to run like hell in front of them shouting, 'This isn't war, it's murder.'

A British officer, 1917.

'Gassed', *the famous painting by war artist John Singer Sargent (1856-1925) depicting men killed and blinded by deadly mustard gas. Because of its indiscriminate effect, gas was never the war-winning weapon its users hoped it would be and neither side deployed it in the Second World War.*

warfare (and, incidentally, gave birth to the tractor that moved like a tank on continuous track). The Nazi Blitzkrieg tactic of the Second World War grew out of the final Allied offensives of 1918, in which tanks, aircraft, artillery and men were carefully co-ordinated.

SIGNS OF HOPE

The human consequences of the war were not all negative. The post-war settlements swept away most of the old autocratic regimes. They were replaced by states that were, at least nominally, democratic republics that upheld human rights.

The war helped bring about the emancipation of women. With so many men in the armed forces, women took over many traditionally male jobs and showed that they could perform them just as well as men. Although not all this new-found emancipation survived after 1918, it was given official recognition in Britain and the USA. In 1918 most women over the age of 30 were given the vote in British parliamentary elections. Two years later the 19th Amendment enfranchised American women.

In the US, black people found jobs that they would not have been offered in peace time. Henry Ford, for example, recruited black people from the South to work in his motor car factory. The migration of black people from the South of America to the North during the war is one of the most significant population shifts of this century.

... the women-workers were doing splendidly. Lads were often selfishly thoughtless, and larked about. The women worked thoughtfully and steadily.

A British priest reporting what he had heard about women factory workers, 1915.

"I Summon you to Comradeship in the Red Cross"

Woodrow Wilson

Posters like this one, drawn by Harrison Fisher in 1918, attracted new recruits into the Red Cross, where they were desperately needed to nurse the casualties of the First World War.

There is evidence that the experience of war helped weaken racial prejudice in some Western nations. Many non-whites in the ranks of the Allies were segregated and given only menial tasks to perform in dreadful conditions. However, units from Africa and Asia also fought in the front line with great valour. The jazz music of the black regiments, enjoyed by units of every race and colour, also helped promote inter-racial understanding.

The war hastened medical advances, too. Doctors treating the horrific casualties of trench warfare learned better ways of wound management and setting fractures. The English doctor Harold Gillies pioneered skin graft surgery. The scale of the medical services required by the war taught doctors and nurses the advantages of specialization and professional hospital management.

MEMORIES AND NEW IDEAS

It took years to come to terms with what had happened during the First World War. As civilization had never experienced anything like it before, people's reactions were as varied as they were horrified.

Many who had taken part never wanted to talk about the war again. Others sought to honour the dead by ensuring that it was never forgotten. Britain instituted a Remembrance Sunday in November, America observed Memorial Day — originally instituted to commemorate the Civil War — and France observed Armistice Day.

On both sides there were those who looked for something or someone to blame for what had happened. The victors accused the Germans, whom they said had started the war. The defeated looked for scapegoats nearer home. Intellectuals questioned pre-war political and economic systems. The hearts and minds of millions seethed with sorrow, shame, bewilderment and rage.

NEW IDEAS

The most dramatic reaction to the war and its effects came in Russia, which experienced two revolutions in 1917. The second brought Lenin's Communist Bolsheviks to power. Following Lenin's pamphlet *Imperialism — The Highest Stage of Capitalism* (1916), Marxist thinkers declared that the war and the misery that went with it had arisen, inevitably, out of capitalist-imperialist competition.

Most people were not too concerned with such abstract thought. Nevertheless, disillusionment with the pre-war style of government helped left-wing parties elsewhere. Communism advanced in Germany and Italy. Britain's first socialist government came to power in 1924. Even the US, the fortress of capitalist democracy, faced an explosion of labour troubles in 1919-1920.

Right-wing movements, too, flourished in the post-war uncertainty. The fascist ex-soldier Benito

Mussolini was appointed prime minister of Italy in 1922. Two years previously the National Socialist (Nazi) Party, with its odd manifesto of racism, popular nationalism and totalitarianism, had appeared in Germany. Italian and German Fascism, therefore, were part of the First World War's confused and bitter legacy.

US president Woodrow Wilson offered a very different reaction to the war when he presented Congress with his famous Fourteen Points on 8 January 1918. Wilson was not concerned with making a new system, but with reforming the old one. His suggestions, which formed the basis of the 1918 Armistice, included redrawing Europe's frontiers along lines of nationality, reducing armaments, free trade and the establishment of an association to protect the independence of all nations.

The optimism of the Fourteen Points was much watered-down in the peace treaties. It found a clearer expression in the Washington Conference that reduced naval armaments and eased tension in the Far East (1921-1922) and the Locarno Treaties that guaranteed European frontiers (1925). The pact outlawing war as a means of diplomacy, drawn up by US Secretary of State Frank B Kellogg, was another example of postwar optimism (1928). It was accepted by a dozen countries, including Germany and the USSR. In the long run, however, both it and the Geneva Disarmament Conference of 1932-1934 were failures.

Pacifism was widely popular among left-wing intellectuals during the 1920s and 1930s. As we will see, reaction to the horrors of 1914-1918 was one reason for the policy of appeasement towards the demands of the Fascist powers in the 1930s. Fear of a second war may in fact have precipitated it.

THE LEAGUE OF NATIONS

Wilson's most original idea was the creation of the League of Nations, established in 1919. Unfortunately, this most idealistic reaction to the First World War was beset with troubles from the start. Crucially, the US

As this Punch *cartoon suggests, President Wilson's hope that the League of Nations would preserve world peace was viewed sceptically even in 1919.*

OVERWEIGHTED.

PRESIDENT WILSON. "HERE'S YOUR OLIVE BRANCH. NOW GET BUSY."
DOVE OF PEACE. "OF COURSE I WANT TO PLEASE EVERYBODY; BUT ISN'T THIS A BIT THICK?"

never joined. Germany was a member only from 1926-1933 and Russia only from 1934-1940. Brazil, Japan and Italy walked out in the face of League criticism. The League had some success in settling minor disputes and in humanitarian work. But as it relied on half-hearted sanctions to enforce its decisions, it proved a toothless tiger.

The League stood for international understanding and security through co-operation. Sadly, such ideas had few supporters in the USA. The first reaction of most Americans, once the war was over, was to leave the rest of the world to its own devices and set about putting their own house in order. Congress refused to ratify the Treaty of Versailles, because it was so harsh on Germany, which was why the world's most powerful country never joined the League of Nations.

THE CULTURE OF WAR

Slaughter made glorious — W B Wollen's painting of Canadian troops repelling a German attack at St Floi, near Ypres, in March 1915.

The First World War did not have an immediate direct impact on popular culture. People wanted to forget the war. When it was mentioned, the tone was either hushed or glorifying the 'brave exploits' of those who had taken part. Dramatic action paintings, such as W B Wollen's showing the Canadians in action at the Battle of Ypres, were preferred to the less romantic work of artists such as J S Sargent or Paul Nash. The hardened ex-soldier 'Bulldog Drummond', who featured in the best-selling novels of H C McNeile, was a typical war hero figure of popular literature. More serious writers and artists tended to be critical of the war. It was almost ten years before the public was ready to accept what they had to say.

The 1920s is often called the 'Jazz Age'. The typical image is of rich young men and women shocking the older generation with their unashamed search for pleasure. Wealthy women threw off the restricting fashions and sexual behaviour of the past. Clubs and bars throbbed to the sensual beat of ragtime and blues. Out went the sedate waltz; in came new dances, such as the uninhibited Charleston. There is some truth in this picture — a frantic attempt to get away from the joylessness of war — but it applied only to the upper classes. Most men and women found escape in more ordinary pursuits: gazing dreamily at the glossy magazines, forgetting reality in an hour or two at the cinema or (illegally in the USA) buying oblivion from the bottle.

Post-war depression lurks behind T S Eliot's poetic masterpiece, *The Waste Land* (1923). But it was another five years before a torrent of new literature about the war appeared. For the first time the world learned what the more sensitive writers had been thinking all along.

Infantry officer Siegfried Sassoon followed his *Memoirs of a Fox-hunting Man* (1928) with *Memoirs of an Infantry Officer* in 1930. By then R C Sherriff's bitter play *Journey's End* had been performed, Robert Graves had published *Goodbye to All That*, Ernest Hemingway had added the American voice with *Farewell to Arms* and Erich Maria Remarque the German voice with *All Quiet on the Western Front* (all 1929).

Together with the tragic poetry of soldiers such as Wilfred Owen, Siegfried Sassoon, Isaac Rosenberg and Edward Thomas, the literature of 1928-1930 formed some of the most powerful writing about war ever to appear. Its universal message was that war was anything but glorious. Its tragedy was that this message was heard by so few.

Wilfred Owen, who died only seven days before the Armistice, wrote some of the most poignant poems of the First World War.

What passing bells for those who die as cattle?
Only the monstrous anger of the guns.
Only the stuttering rifles' rapid rattle
Can patter out their hasty orisons.
No mockeries now for them; no prayers nor bells;
Nor any voice of mourning save the choirs, -
The shrill demented choirs of wailing shells;
And bugles calling for them from sad shires.

From *Anthem for Doomed Youth* by Wilfred Owen.

A NEW MAP OF EUROPE

Four great empires collapsed as a consequence of the First World War. The Russian Empire fell apart in 1917. By the time the war ended, the days of the Austro-Hungarian Empire were also numbered. Its division into several smaller nations was arranged at the Treaties of St Germain (1919) and Trianon (1920). The final collapse of the Ottoman Empire was confirmed in 1920 by the Treaty of Sèvres. In 1919 the fate of the German Empire was negotiated in Paris and sealed in the Palace of Versailles, France — precisely where it had been announced 48 years before.

The disappearance of the empires led to the reappearance of old countries, the creation of new ones and the alteration of many existing boundaries. The result of all these changes was a political map of Europe that looked radically different from that of 1914.

RUSSIA

Had there been no First World War, the Russian Empire might have survived well into the twentieth century. In 1914 the Russian economy was booming. Although opposed (sometimes violently) by groups ranging from Liberals to Communists, the government of Tsar Nicholas II had survived an attempted revolution (1905) and still kept the loyalty of the bulk of Russians. The war shattered this loyalty for ever.

The humiliating defeats of 1914 were followed by further German advances and costly campaigns against Austria-Hungary. The Russian forces were ill-fed, under-equipped and poorly led. By January 1917 mutiny was widespread. When strikes and rioting broke out in Petrograd (St Petersburg) in March 1917, troops sided with the opposition. The tsar abdicated and a Provisional Government took over the country.

... the October [Soviet] revolution inflicted a mortal wound on world capitalism from which ... [it] will never recover .... The era of the 'stability' of capitalism has passed away, taking with it the legend of the indestructibility of the bourgeois order.
The era of the collapse of capitalism has begun.

Joseph Stalin, secretary of the Soviet Communist Party, 1927.

Russian famine victims, 1922. In some parts of the country starvation forced people to cannibalism.

Keen to keep in with the Western democracies, the Provisional Government pressed on with the unpopular war. The chaos and losses continued. Hoping he would stir up trouble for the new government, the Germans allowed Communist leader Lenin to return to Russia from Switzerland via Germany. The hope became a reality in November 1917 when Lenin's Communists seized power in Petrograd. After three years of starvation and slaughter, the Communists' simple slogan of 'Peace, Bread, Land' had wide popular appeal. Peace came at the Treaty of Brest-Litovsk. Bread and land were harder to secure.

The 'Reds', or Communists, and the 'Whites', or anti-Communists, fought a long and bloody civil war. By the time the Reds had won in November 1922, Finland, Estonia, Latvia, Lithuania and Poland had emerged as independent nations. The Union of Soviet Socialist Republics (USSR), dominated by Russia, controlled most of the rest of the old tsarist empire. The setting up of the world's first Communist state in so vast and powerful a country as Russia began a new phase in world history. It was without doubt the most startling and important consequence of the First World War.

AUSTRIA-HUNGARY

Herr Habsburg, the taxi is waiting.

The socialist leader Karl Renner to Charles I, the last of the Austrian emperors as he went into exile, 1918.

In 1914 the old-fashioned Austro-Hungarian Empire was like a state caught in a time warp. It was not a nation but a group of territories held together by the rule of the Habsburg dynasty. When it fell, therefore, its various parts broke away to become independent nations. The last emperor, Charles I, abdicated in 1918 and Austria became a republic. The new government immediately voted for union, or *anschluss* with Germany, but this was forbidden by the victorious powers meeting in Versailles. The Austrians were frustrated by this ruling. As a result, many of them welcomed the Austro-German *anschluss* of 1938, when Austria was annexed by Nazi Germany.

The Treaty of St Germain set up the new state of Czechoslovakia and gave South Tyrol to Italy. This left Austria without direct access to the sea. She was also saddled with high reparation payments and forbidden to maintain an army of more than 30 thousand.

The Treaty of Trianon reduced the size of Hungary by three-fifths. This cut her population from

Europe reconstructed. The old empires of Germany, Russia, Austria-Hungary and Turkey were replaced by a jig-saw puzzle of small nations.

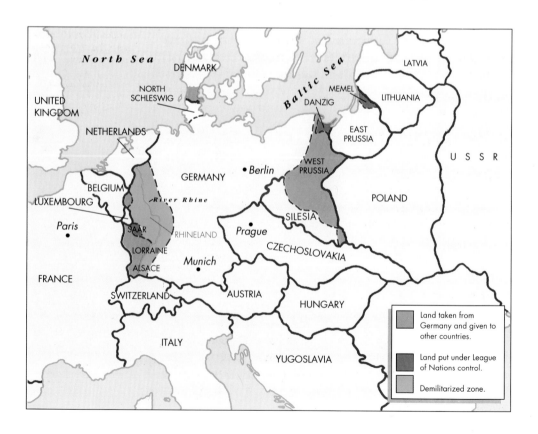

21 to 8 million. Land in the west went to Czechoslovakia and in the east to another 'manu-factured' new country, Yugoslavia. Romania gained the region of Transylvania. Like the Austrians, the Hungarians were deeply unhappy at the way they had been treated and during the 1930s and they sided with the Fascists. Bulgaria's fate was settled by the Treaty of Neuilly (1919). She was forced to give territory to Greece, Yugoslavia and Romania and was left with no port on the Mediterranean.

THE OTTOMAN EMPIRE

The Allies used the break up of the Ottoman Empire to extend their influence in the Middle East. Syria, Transjordan, Iraq and Palestine were declared 'man-dates' under the control of the League of Nations. As the League had no machinery of government, France took control of Syria and Britain the remaining three mandates.

Palestine gave Britain a headache of her own making. During the war, in order to win Arab support against Turkey, she had made vague promises of Palestine becoming part of an independent Arab state. In 1917, however, Foreign Secretary Arthur Balfour had offered British support for an independent Jewish state in the region. The two proposals were obviously contradictory. They signalled the start of decades of bitter Arab-Jewish conflict.

The Treaty of Sèvres gave the Turkish province of Smyrna to Greece and set up a Republic of Armenia. Both moves were rejected by the nationalists in the new Turkish republic and a Graeco-Turkish war broke out. The terms of the Treaty of Sèvres were revised in Turkey's favour at Lausanne: the independent Armenia ceased to exist, but not Armenian aspira-tions, which have yet to be fulfilled.

His Majesty's Government views with favour the establishment in Palestine of a nat-ional home for the Jewish people, and will use their best endeavours to facili-tate the achievement of this object.

From the Balfour declaration, 2 November 1917.

GERMANY AND VERSAILLES

In 1919 the popular cry among the victors was to 'squeeze the German lemon until the pips squeak'. The result was a treaty so hostile that it stood little chance of being the basis for a lasting peace. The German representatives at Versailles had to sign it without negotiation.

German children play with money made worthless by galloping inflation after the War.

The treaty stated that Germany had started the war. She gave back Alsace and Lorraine to France. Silesia went to Czechoslovakia and other territory was given to Belgium and Lithuania. The majority of the peoples in all these areas were German-speaking. Poland picked up German territory in the east. The key Baltic port of Danzig, the industrial region of the Saar and the strategically important Rhineland, were also taken from Germany. Her armed forces were strictly limited and her colonies made League of Nations mandates. Finally, in 1921 a Reparations Commission decided that Germany should pay £6,500 million (132 billion gold marks) compensation to the Allies for the damage she had caused.

What a use could be made of the Treaty of Versailles! ... How each one of the points of that Treaty could be branded in the minds and hearts of the German people until sixty million men and women find their souls aflame with a feeling of rage and shame.

Adolf Hitler in *Mein Kampf*, 1925.

The Treaty of Versailles left Germany humiliated and impoverished. Its new government, the Weimar Republic, was immediately unpopular because it had accepted the peace settlement. (It had no choice, of course). For five years the Republic struggled to exist. There were attempted coups from both the left and the right. Unemployment rarely fell below 10 per cent of the workforce and in 1926 it soared to almost 20 per cent. From 1923-1929 Belgian and French troops occupied the Ruhr when Germany fell behind with her reparation payments. Soaring inflation destroyed savings and made serious economic planning impossible: by the autumn of 1923 a single US dollar was worth 4.2 trillion marks.

To help Germany with her difficulties, in 1924 US banker Charles G Dawes devised a plan to lighten the burden of reparation payments. By 1928 a degree of stability had returned to the German economy. Nevertheless, many Germans were still bitter about how they had been treated. When the country was thrown into chaos by the world-wide recession of the early 1930s, a large part of the electorate turned to the party that condemned Versailles as a 'lie'. In 1933 the leader of this party, Adolf Hitler, became his country's Nazi chancellor. The following year he was proclaimed 'Führer of the German Reich'.

The most terrifying consequence of all — Adolf Hitler speaking at a political rally in 1930s Germany. Nazi condemnation of the Treaty of Versailles was a key plank in Hitler's populist manifesto.

British prime minister Lloyd George had thought the Versailles terms unnecessarily harsh. 'We shall have to fight another war all over again in 25 years time,' he declared in 1919, 'at three times the cost.' His prophesy was out by five years.

NEW NATIONS

Not everyone rejected the post-war settlements. The chance for self-government brought new hopes and aspirations to millions of Europeans. Sadly, it also brought new problems. The history of the democratic states set up by the Paris Peace Conference makes depressing reading.

As we have seen, Armenia disappeared almost before the ink on the Treaty of Sèvres was dry. The conflicting hopes of Arabs and Jews led to years of unrest in Palestine. Democracy did not survive long in the Baltic republics of Latvia, Estonia and Lithuania. By the 1930s all three were in the grip of right-wing regimes. Poland was a virtual dictatorship by 1926. Democracy re-emerged in all four countries only after the collapse of European Communism (1989 onwards).

The history of Yugoslavia (not officially called such until 1929) was even more unhappy. Welding the Serbs, Croats and Slovenes — Christian and Muslim — into a single nation was a near-impossible task. After 1927 the country was united by a royal autocracy. In the Second World War it fell to the Communists. During the 1990s it dissolved into a civil war of horrifying barbarity. During the last decade of the century, the world's attention was as firmly focused on the Balkans as it had been during the first decade. As far as the people living there were concerned, the First World War solved nothing.

Of all the new states established after the First World War, only Finland and Czechoslovakia survived as democratic republics throughout the interwar period. Both then suffered greatly during the mid-century turmoil. After long years of Soviet domination, in 1990 Czechoslovakia divided peacefully into the Czech and Slovak Republics.

In 1918 President Wilson had hoped for a settlement to make the world 'fit and safe to live in ... and safe for every peace-loving nation which ... wishes to live its own life....' Time showed that high hopes and fair words were not enough to make his dream come true.

Your treaty [Mr President] means injustice. It means slavery. It means war. And to all this you ask this republic to become a party. You ask it to abandon the creed under which it has grown to power and accept the creed of autocracy, the creed of repression and force.

Senator Wilhelm E Borah speaking against Congressional ratification of the Treaty of Versailles in 1919.

THE VICTORS AT PEACE

The First World War had an enormous impact on the victorious nations. Most significantly, it changed for ever the relationship between them. By 1918 British debts to the US totalled a staggering $3,696 million. France owed almost $2 billion and Italy just over $1 billion. By 1922 the total Allied debt to the US had soared to some $11.5 billion dollars. The USA was both the most powerful nation in the world and its largest creditor. The twentieth century was now the American Century.

THE USA

Joining a European war had been a dramatic break with the American tradition. So had the federal government's direction of every aspect of the war effort. Understandably, once the war was over there was a clamour for the clock to be put back to its pre-war position. The military was reduced to peace time levels, industry handed back to private ownership and a limit on naval armaments negotiated.

US workers on a federal works program in 1935. Economic stability was destroyed by the war. After a decade of fluctuation, the world economy plunged into depression in 1929, forcing governments everywhere to set up emergency relief programmes.

Nevertheless, things did not return to quite where they had stood before. The privatized railroads, for example, were subject to strict new controls. The federal government's wartime powers had set a precedent, too. In the 1930s, when the nation faced the crisis of the Great Depression, it was to the federal government that people turned once more for leadership. The roots of President Franklin D Roosevelt's New Deal lay in the powers taken by his Democrat predecessor President Wilson during the First World War.

After a brief post-war dip, the US economy flourished. This did not fill the average American with goodwill towards either their leaders or foreigners. The electorate was tired of the Democrats' meddling in international affairs. They also complained that the cost of living was too high. As a result, in 1920 they chose as president the conservative Republican Warren G Harding. The same mood of disillusionment led the Senate to reject the Treaty of Versailles. In the South it bred racial violence, often stirred by the hateful Ku Klux Klan (inactive since the 1870s and reborn in 1915).

Americans had expected too much from the war. It had brought them some glory, but it had also cost over 100 thousand American lives and fed a rapid rise in the cost of living. So much, they thought, for getting

A new member is welcomed into the Ku Klux Klan, 1922. The right-wing, racist Klan was an ugly manifestation of the intolerant isolationism that swept the US immediately after the war.

mixed up in matters that were really no concern of theirs. Aggressive isolation was now their watchword.

After the success of the Communists in Russia, an illogical 'Red Scare' swept the US in 1919-1920. Russians, Germans, Italians — anyone vaguely suspicious was targeted. Mistrust of foreigners produced a series of measures to cut immigration (1921-1924) and the Fordney-McCumber Tariff (1922), which placed heavy duties on many imports.

But as the world's leading economic power, it was not possible for America to cut itself off completely. US financial interests in Europe required Dawes to reschedule Germany's reparation payments and reorganize her State Bank (see pages 60-61). Another US businessman, Owen D Young, headed the committee that rearranged the reparation payments a second time in 1929.

The Washington Conference of 1921-1922 confirmed that the US had taken on the role of policing the Pacific — and beyond. The agreements reached at Washington settled for the moment the tension between the US and Japan that had arisen out of the war. But in signing the Nine-Power Pact (1922) that guaranteed China's independence, the US set off down a path that would eventually lead her to war again.

> The business of the United States is business .... The man who builds a factory builds a temple. The man who works there worships there.
>
> President Calvin Coolidge, 1925.

BRITAIN AND FRANCE

In Britain and France the end of the war was greeted with scenes of wild rejoicing. The French celebrated more than just the end of a terrible slaughter. They had got revenge for the humiliating German defeat of 1870-1871 and retaken Alsace and Lorraine. The French army was the toast of Europe. A French soldier, Marshal Foch, had been accepted as Allied Commander-in-Chief and led the successful offensives of 1918. When Paris was chosen to host the peace negotiations, it was a sign that, for the time being at least, the capital of France was the capital of Europe.

The joy of victory masked serious problems. France had lost a higher proportion of her armed forces than any other major Allied power. The slow birth-rate during the inter-war years meant that by 1939 her population was no larger than in 1913. A huge swathe of northern and eastern France, the line of the Western Front, had been completely devastated. To this day it is still possible to trace the line of the

An Irish postcard entitled 'The Birth of the Irish Republic'. The 1916 Easter Rising was easily quashed by British troops. However, in 1919 civil war broke out in Ireland and two years later the country was divided between the British north and the Irish south. The settlement remains a source of anguish to this day.

trenches on a map by its absence of towns and villages.

Wartime inflation did not blow away with the smoke of the guns. To meet the cost of the war, the French government had printed money, thereby reducing its value. In 1914 $1US was worth about 5 French francs. By 1923 the figure had risen to FF 16.5 and by 1926 to FF 26.5. Nevertheless, the French economy performed quite well in the 1920s. It was helped by reparation payments and the wealth taken when French troops occupied the German industrial district of the Ruhr in 1923.

Unlike the French, the British had few tangible gains to show for their victory. As the war drew to a close, a feeling arose that the country had been fighting not just to end German militarism but to create a 'better Britain'. The mood was caught by the coalition government. It promised, among other things, a massive housing programme: 'homes fit for heroes'.

The homes were never built. After a brief upturn, the British economy entered a decade of uncertainty and slow growth. By 1921 unemployment stood at 23 per cent. In the same year exports to the US fell by almost 43 per cent. Government spending was cut back and in 1924 the country was halted by a General Strike. The Labour Government of 1924, pledged to uphold the cause of the working man and woman, seemed no more capable of tackling the country's problems than had its Conservative and Liberal opponents.

Britain's problems were not confined to domestic matters. In 1916 the Irish had taken advantage of the war to launch an Easter Rising against their imperial masters. Civil War flared in 1919 and in 1921 the country was divided between the British north and an Irish Free State in the south. In the colonies, particularly India, the feeling grew that the peoples who had fought beside each other should now be treated as equals. Independence movements sprouted and there was active resistance to British rule in India, Egypt, Iraq and Palestine.

Disillusion seeped into the hearts and minds of the British people. For what had they sacrificed their young men and endured four years of hardship and deprivation? For misery and decline? Fifteen years after the Armistice, the students of the Oxford University Union voted by 275 to 153 that 'this House will in no circumstances fight for its King and Country'.

ITALY AND JAPAN

Italy's armed forces had not covered themselves in glory during the First World War. Things did not improve at the peace conferences, either. Italy did not get all the Austrian territory she had hoped for. More irritating, she received neither Albania nor the territory she wanted in Dalmatia.

The war devastated Italy's economy. As well as massive debts to the US, she faced roaring inflation (the value of the lira fell from 5 to $1US in 1914 to 28 to $1US in 1921). The cost of living rose five-fold and unemployment escalated out of control. Membership of non-democratic Communist and right-wing parties grew. A wave of strikes, accompanied by violence and looting, rocked the country.

The country's unstable liberal democracy could not cope. In October 1922 King Victor Emmanuel II invited the Fascist leader Benito Mussolini to form a government. During the 1920s Mussolini did away with the system that had brought him to power and established a totalitarian dictatorship. For Italy the fruits of the war were bitter indeed.

Japan, on the other hand, did well out of the war. Her cotton cloth exports trebled and the tonnage of her merchant fleet doubled. But the boom ended with peace and during the 1920s the country experienced the sort of unemployment and industrial unrest that troubled most other industrial nations. Despite these problems, democratic government survived and was strengthened by widening the electorate. When Japan joined the Council of the League of Nations and attended the Washington Conference, it was clear she had been accepted as a co-operative member of the community of nations. Only the rumbling discontent of the military and right-wing politicians suggested a bleaker future.

We danced on the buses, we danced on the lorries, we danced on the pavement, we shouted, we sang .... [The] office boys and girls at the War Office yelled to their companions across the way; we cheered and cheered again and again, while church bells rang out a peal of jubilation.

Sir Evelyn Wrench, recalling the euphoria of Armistice Day in London, 1918.

Fascism is not only a party, it is a regime; it is not only a regime but a faith; it is not only a faith but a religion.

Benito Mussolini, 1933.

THE FAILURE OF THE PEACEMAKERS

In September 1939, almost exactly 21 years after the ending of the First World War, Europe went to war again. It is customary, therefore, to consider the First and Second World Wars as part of the same struggle. From a European point of view they appear almost two halves of the same civil war. Even in 1919 there were many who predicted that the Versailles settlement would be merely a 'cease-fire'.

In the light of what happened in 1939, it is easy to say that the post-war settlements were doomed to failure. Yet it can be argued that the causes of the Second World War can be found almost entirely in the events of the 1920s and 1930s. Why, in other words, did the 'war to end all war' not end all war?

THE WEAKNESSES OF THE TREATIES

The Treaties include nothing to make the defeated Central Empires into good neighbours, nothing to stabilize the new States of Europe, nothing to reclaim Russia ....

John Maynard Keynes, British economist, 1920.

The weaknesses of the Treaty of Versailles, the most important of the post-war settlements, lay in the fact that it was a compromise. The French wished to make sure that Germany could never threaten the peace of Europe again. They wanted the country divided and completely demilitarized. This would have left France in the position it had been in before 1870 — the most powerful military nation in Western Europe.

The Americans, and to a lesser extent the British, would not tolerate such harsh treatment of their former enemy. In his Fourteen Points President Wilson said he wanted all peoples to be free to settle their own destinies. He did not make an exception of the Germans and the German government agreed to a cease-fire in the belief that the German people would be free to decide their own future.

The Versailles Treaty came out somewhere between the French and Anglo-American positions. Germany remained the most populous and economically powerful country on the continent. But she was infuriated by the way some German-speakers were dispersed to other countries. She detested the Treaty's 'war guilt' clause. The scale of reparations, she claimed, was unjust. So was her disarmament and the way she was given no say in the Treaty's terms.

Versailles left Germany bowed but not broken. Just as the defeat of 1870-1871 had left the French dreaming of revenge, so Versailles left many Germans with similar dreams in 1919.

The other weaknesses of the settlements were perhaps less obvious. There was no way of knowing how the new nations

The famous Fourteen Points of President Wilson, presented to Congress in January 1918. It was on the basis of these points that Germany accepted the Armistice in November 1918.

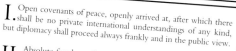

Program for the Peace of the World
By PRESIDENT WILSON January 8, 1918

I. Open covenants of peace, openly arrived at, after which there shall be no private international understandings of any kind, but diplomacy shall proceed always frankly and in the public view.

II. Absolute freedom of navigation upon the seas, outside territorial waters, alike in peace and in war, except as the seas may be closed in whole or in part by international action for the enforcement of international covenants.

III. The removal, so far as possible, of all economic barriers and the establishment of an equality of trade conditions among all the nations consenting to the peace and associating themselves for its maintenance.

IV. Adequate guarantees given and taken that national armaments will reduce to the lowest point consistent with domestic safety.

V. Free, open-minded, and absolutely impartial adjustment of all colonial claims, based upon a strict observance of the principle that in determining all such questions of sovereignty the interests of the population concerned must have equal weight with the equitable claims of the government whose title is to be determined.

VI. The evacuation of all Russian territory and such a settlement of all questions affecting Russia as will secure the best and freest co-operation of the other nations of the world in obtaining for her an unhampered and unembarassed opportunity for the independent determination of her own political development and national policy, and assure her of a sincere welcome into the society of free nations under institutions of her own choosing; and, more than a welcome, assistance also of every kind that she may need and may herself desire. The treatment accorded Russia by her sister nations in the months to come will be the acid test of their goodwill, of their comprehension of her needs as distinguished from their own interests, and of their intelligent and unselfish sympathy.

VII. Belgium, the whole world will agree, must be evacuated and restored, without any attempt to limit the sovereignty which she enjoys in common with all other free nations. No other single act will serve as this will serve to restore confidence among the nations in the law which they have themselves set and determined for the government of their relations

with one another. Without this healing act the whole structure and validity of international law is forever impaired.

VIII. All French territory should be freed and the invaded portions restored, and the wrong done to France by Prussia in 1871 in the matter of Alsace-Lorraine, which has unsettled the peace of the world for nearly fifty years, should be righted, in order that peace may once more be made secure in the interest of all.

IX. A readjustment of the frontiers of Italy should be effected along clearly recognisable lines of nationality.

X. The people of Austria-Hungary, whose place among the nations we wish to see safeguarded and assured, should be accorded the freest opportunity of autonomous development.

XI. Rumania, Serbia and Montenegro should be evacuated; occupied territories restored; Serbia accorded free and secure access to the sea; and the relations of the several Balkan States to one another determined by friendly counsel along historically established lines of allegiance and nationality; and international guarantees of political and economic independence and territorial integrity of the several Balkan States should be entered into.

XII. The Turkish portions of the present Ottoman Empire should be assured a secure sovereignty, but the other nationalities which are now under Turkish rule should be assured an undoubted security of life and an absolutely unmolested opportunity of autonomous development, and the Dardanelles should be permanently opened as a free passage to the ships and commerce of all nations under international guarantees.

XIII. An independent Polish state should be erected which should include the territories inhabited by indisputably Polish populations, which should be assured a free and secure access to the sea, and whose political and economic independence and territorial integrity should be guaranteed by international covenant.

XIV. A general association of nations must be formed under specific covenants for the purpose of affording mutual guarantees of political independence and territorial integrity to great and small States alike.

were going to behave, although it was wildly optimistic to believe the Balkan problem could be solved by turning Serbia into a multi-ethnic Yugoslavia. Italy's slide into dictatorship had as much to do with the country's internal problems as with post-war disappointment. The Palestinian situation was the result of Britain's wartime diplomacy rather than her government of the mandate. The League of Nations was a noble, if unrealistic idea. Its creators cannot be blamed for the way ruthless governments ignored it. Nor were they to know that the US Senate would reject it from the outset.

UNSOLVED PROBLEMS

The Treaty's weaknesses made a second war a possibility, but by no means inevitable. Three further consequences of the war, however, did make it a likelihood. The first was the legacy of bitterness that led the French to continue their struggle with Germany by occupying the Ruhr in 1923. This was the vast Essen steel works, which France feared might once again become a centre for the production of armaments. The occupation led to a loss of production and fed the inflation that was undermining Germany's wealth and morale. At a time when peace needed to be given a chance, French action rekindled German hatred of their wartime enemy. If there were Germans who had accepted the Versailles settlement as just, the occupation of the Rhur almost guaranteed that they would change their minds.

When the Nazis got control of Germany, they openly defied the Treaty of Versailles. In 1936, for example, Hitler sent troops into the demilitarized Rhineland. The reaction in the countries which had dictated the treaty was dangerously hesitant. Instead of acting firmly, they followed a

In June 1919 the Treaty of Versailles was signed in the Hall of Mirrors, Versailles, where the German Empire had been proclaimed in January 1871. The venue was deliberately chosen to humiliate the German signatories, who had been allowed no say in the Treaty's content.

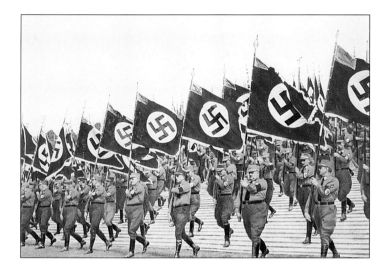

Nazi brownshirts parade at Nuremburg, 1933. In 1919 the eventual re-emergence of German militarism was predicted by those who criticized the harsh terms of the Treaty of Versailles.

policy of appeasement. This meant giving way to the Fascists' lesser demands in the hope of preventing greater demands in future.

Appeasement arose partly out of military unpreparedness. But its roots also went back to the First World War and the Treaty of Versailles. Knowing the history of their century only too well, the leaders of the European democracies had a horror of war. They also felt a lingering guilt at the harsh way Germany had been treated in the period following the Armistice.

Finally, the world economy never fully recovered from the turmoil of world war. US reluctance to take over Britain's role as manager of the world economy left a worrying vacuum. After the Second World War the US poured money into Europe to prop up the shaky democracies. If she had followed a similar policy in the 1920s, the economy of Europe might have been put on a more secure footing. Perhaps this would have saved the world from the nightmare of Fascism. But Republican presidents were not prepared to say where US dollars should go. High US tariffs limited a European recovery and a high proportion of US investment went to Latin America.

The Dawes and Young Plans were steps in the right direction, but no more. So when the world plunged into recession in 1929, the fragile German democracy was unable to resist the bitter Nazi tide. The Communists had come to power as a direct result of the First World War. The Nazis emerged out of postwar gloom and discontent. The two terrible regimes made sure that the consequences of the First World War lasted well into the second half of the century.

We regard the Munich Agreement as a sign of the desire of our two peoples never to go to war with one another again.

Adolf Hitler and Neville Chamberlain, 1938. In the Munich agreement, Czechoslovakian Sudetenland was handed over to Germany.

GLOSSARY

Allies
Britain, France, Russia, Italy, the USA and the other countries that fought in alliance with them during the First World War.

Alliance
A bond or treaty made between countries to further their common interests.

Annex
To occupy and take over territory formerly belonging to another power.

Armistice
An agreement to cease fighting, bringing a war to an end.

Archduke
A prince of the Austrian royal family.

Assassinate
Murder a major political or military figure.

Autocracy
A country in which the government has absolute power.

Balkans
South-eastern Europe, including Romania, Bulgaria, Albania, Greece and former Yugoslavia.

Blockade
The blocking of a harbour to prevent supplies being delivered to it.

Bolsheviks
The group of Communists that seized power in Russia in 1917.

Boom
A period of sudden, swift economic development.

Capitalism
Economic system by which the means of production, distribution and exchange are privately owned and there is a minimum of government direction.

Central Powers
Germany and its allies in the First World War.

Civil War
War fought between the people of one country.

Coalition
A government made up of members from more than one party.

Colonies
Overseas territories conquered and governed by another country.

Communism
Political system by which all property is collectively owned and the State takes control of nearly every aspect of life.

Conscription
Compulsory military service.

Convoy
Many merchant ships sailing together for protection.

Dardanelles
The southernmost end of the sea passage from the Mediterranean to the Black Sea.

Demilitarize
To withdraw all armed forces.

Democracy
Government by the people or their elected representatives.

Diplomacy
Discussion between states.

Eastern Front
The battle front between Russia and the Central Powers.

Economy
A country's finances, services and industry.

Empire
A widespread group of colonies, under the same government.

Entente
A friendly agreement between states.

Exports
Goods produced in one country and sold abroad.

Fascism
An absolute political system stressing the importance of nationalism and the country's leader.

Foreign Policy
A state's policy towards other countries.

Free Trade
International trade without customs duties.

Imperial
Relating to an empire.

Imports
The goods that a country buys from abroad.

Inflation
The falling value of money.

Kaiser
The Emperor of Germany.

Left Wing
Tending towards Socialism or liberalism.

Liberal
A political belief that emphasizes the rights of the individual.

Mobilize
To prepare armed forces for war.

Nationalism
A strong, patriotic feeling and a desire to make one's country independent.

Nazi
Member of the National Socialist German Workers Party, which came to power under Adolf Hitler.

Neutral
Not taking sides in a dispute.

Occupy
To take over a state or territory.

Ottoman Empire
The Turkish Empire.

Panslavism
The movement to unite all peoples of the Slavic race.

Propaganda
Information (sometimes false) designed to promote a single point of view.

Recession
Economic downturn.

Reparations
Payment to the victors by the defeated country to meet the cost of the war.

Republic
Country without a monarch but with an elected head of state.

Revolution
Complete and rapid change.

Right Wing
Inclined towards capitalism and, in its extreme form, Fascism.

Sanctions
Non-violent action taken by one state to encourage another state to do something.

Slav
Member of any of the peoples of Eastern Europe or Soviet Asia.

Slump
Deep recession.

Socialism
The political system that stresses welfare and equality above profit and individualism.

Soviet
Used to describe anything relating to the former USSR.

Treaty
A written agreement between nations.

Ultimatum
A final demand, the rejection of which might lead to war.

Unification
The creation of one country from a number of smaller ones.

Western Front
The front line of hostilities during the First World War, running through France and Belgium.

TIMELINE

1815 — European leaders meet at the Congress of Vienna to discuss the future of Europe after the defeat of France's emperor, Napoleon I.

1854-1856 — The Crimean War is fought in Russia.

1870 — Prussia defeats France in the Franco-Prussian War (until 1871).

1871 — The new German Empire is proclaimed at Versailles.

1872 — The League of Three Emperors is formed between Germany, Russia and Austria-Hungary.

1879 — Germany and Austria-Hungary create the Dual Alliance.

1882 — Italy forms a Triple Alliance with Germany and Austria-Hungary.

1887 — A Reinsurance Treaty is signed, by which Russia and Germany agree not to go to war with each other.

1888 — Wilhelm II succeeds as emperor of Germany.

1890 — Otto von Bismarck resigns.

1894 — France and Russia are linked in a Dual Alliance.

1897 — Austria-Hungary and Russia agree to co-operate in order to maintain peace in the Balkans.

1898 — A short war known as the Fashoda Crisis breaks out between Britain and France in the Sudan.
— The first German Navy Law announces a massive expansion of the German fleet
— An American battleship is destroyed at Havana, Cuba, provoking the Spanish-American War.

1899 — Britain is at war with the Boer republics of the Orange Free State and the Transvaal in southern Africa (until 1902).

1902 — The Anglo-Japanese Alliance is formed, by which the two countries agree to oppose Russian claims in northern China.
— Civil war breaks out in Morocco.

1904 — Britain and France sign the *entente cordiale.*

1904-1905 — Russia and Japan go to war over Korea.

1905 — Germany's Schlieffen Plan of attack is finalized.
— The first Moroccan crisis occurs, provoked by Kaiser Wilhelm II's visit to the country.

1906 — The Algeciras Conference confims French rights in Morocco.
— The first Dreadnought class of battleship is launched by the British navy.

1907 — A Triple Entente between Britain, Russia and France is formed.

1908 — Austria-Hungary annexes the largely Serb provinces of Bosnia and Herzegovina.

1911 — A second Moroccan crisis is provoked by Germany sending a gunboat to Agadir.

1912 — The First Balkan War in which the Ottoman Turks are defeated by the Balkan League.

1913 — The First Balkan War is concluded by the Treaty of London.
— The Second Balkan War breaks out, in which Bulgaria is defeated by her former allies, Serbia, Greece and Montenegro.

1914 — **June** Archduke Franz Ferdinand, heir to the Austro-Hungarian Empire, is assassinated at Sarajevo, Bosnia.
— **July** Austria-Hungary declares war on Serbia.
— Russia mobilizes its troops to defend Serbia.
— **August** Germany declares war on Russia.
— Germany declares war on France and invades Belgium.
— World War breaks out when Britain declares war on Germany.
— Japan joins Allies.
— **November** Turkey joins Germany and Austria-Hungary.

1915 — **February** Germany begins

unrestricted submarine warfare.
— **May** Italy joins the Allies.

1916 — The Arabs revolt against their Turkish overlords.
— Woodrow Wilson is re-elected as US president.

1917 — **January** Germany reintroduces unrestricted submarine warfare.
— The Bolshevik Communists come to power in Russia after over-throwing the government of the Tsar.
— **April** The USA declares war on Germany.

1918 — **January** US president Woodrow Wilson announces 14 Points.
— **March** Russia and Germany sign the Treaty of Brest-Litovsk.
— The French soldier Marshal Foch becomes Allied Commander-in-Chief on Western Front.
— **November** Austria-Hungary signs the armistice.
— Armistice on Western Front.

1919 — **January** The Paris Peace Conference meets to bring a formal end to the war.
— **June** The Treaty of Versailles is signed by Germany and the Allies.
— **September** The Austrians sign the Treaty of St Germain, bringing an end to the Habsburg monarchy.
— **November** The Treaty of Neuilly is signed, by which Bulgaria is forced to give territory to Greece, Yugoslavia and Romania.
— US Senate rejects Treaty of Versailles.

1920 — **June** The Austro-Hungarian Empire is broken up under the Treaty of Trianon.
— **August** The Allies and Turkey sign the Treaty of Sèvres, by which the remains of the Ottoman Empire is broken up.

1921 — The figures for German reparation payments are fixed.
— Washington Conference (to 1922) is held to discuss the reduction of naval weapons.

1922 — Mussolini becomes Prime Minister of Italy.

1923 — French and Belgian troops occupy the Ruhr (to 1929).

1924 — The US banker Charles G Dawes devises a plan to lighten the burden of German reparation payments.

1925 — The Locarno Pact settles European frontiers.

1926 — Germany joins the League of Nations.

1928 — The Kellogg-Briand Pact denounces war.

1929 — The Young Plan to ease German reparations further is presented.
— Wall Street Crash signals a world-wide economic collapse.

1932 — The Disarmament Conference meets at Geneva.

1933 — Adolf Hitler becomes Chancellor of Germany, which leaves the League of Nations.
— Japan leaves the League of Nations.

FURTHER READING

BOOKS SUITABLE FOR SCHOOL STUDENTS

Briggs, A, et al (eds), *Andromeda Oxford History of the Twentieth Century*, 8 vols., Abingdon 1993.

Bridge, F R, *The Coming of the First World War*, Historical Association, London, 1985.

Henig, R, *The Origins of the First World War*, 2nd edit, 1993.

Henig, R, *Versailles and After*, 2nd edit., Routledge, London, 1995.

Longman Chronicle of the Twentieth Century, Longman, London, 1988, updated annually.

Martel, G, *The Origins of the First World War*, 1987.

Overy, R J, *The Inter-war Crisis, 1919-39*, Longman, London, 1994.

Remarque, E M, *All Quiet on the Western Front*, Routledge, London, 1988.

Ross, S, *Causes and Consequences of the Second World War*, Evans Brothers Ltd, London, 1995.

Ross, S, *The Origins of the First World War*, Wayland, Hove, 1988.

Williamson, D, *War and Peace: International Relations 1914-1945*, Hodder and Stoughton, London, 1994.

ADULT BOOKS

Decondes, A, *An Encyclopaedia of American Foreign Policy*, vol. 2, 3rd edit, Charles Scribner's Sons, New York, 1978.

Fearon, P, *War, Prosperity and Depression: The US Economy, 1917-1945*, Lawrence and Wishart, London, 1987.

Joll, J, *The Origins of the First World War*, Longman, London, 1984.

Kennedy, P, *The Rise and Fall of the Great Powers*, Unwin Hyman, London, 1988.

Northedge, F S, *The League of Nations: its Life and Times*, Leicester University Press, Leicester, 1986.

Pratt, J W, *America and World Leadership 1900-1921*, Collier-Macmillan, New York, 1967.

Stevenson, D, *The First World War and International Politics*, OUP, Oxford, 1991.

Taylor, A J P, *The Struggle for the Mastery of Europe*, OUP, Oxford, 1971.

INDEX

Acknowledgements

The publishers are grateful to the following for permission to reproduce photographs:

The Mary Evans Picture Library, pages 7, 13, 17, 19, 22, 24, 25, 26, 29, 47, 53; Corbis-Bettmann, page 63; E T Archive, cover, pages 10, 15, 38, 39, 43, 48, 50, 61; The Hulton Getty Picture Collection, pages 37, 57, 64; Image Select, page 28, 44; Image Select/Ann Ronan page 60; Peter Newark's Western Americana, pages 8, 21, 30, 36, 40, 41, 42, 46, 51, 54, 66, 70, 71; Popperfoto, pages 33, 45.